Street by Street

IPSWICH

FELIXSTOWE, HADLEIGH, NEEDHAM MARKET, STOWMARKET, WOODBRIDGE

Bramford, Brantham, Capel St Mary, East Bergholt, Great Blakenham, Grundisburgh, Kesgrave, Kirton, Martlesham Heath, Shotley Gate, Sproughton, Trimley St Mary, Washbrook, Wickham Market

2nd edition March 2008

Original edition printed February 2003

Enabled by | Ordnance Survey

© Automobile Association Developments Limited 2008

Published by AA Publishing (a trading name of Automobile Association Developments Limited, whose registered office is Fanum House, Basing View, Basingstoke, Hampshire RG21 4EA. Registered number 1878835).

Produced by the Mapping Services Department of The Automobile Association. (A03561)

A CIP Catalogue record for this book is available from the British Library.

Printed by Oriental Press in Dubai

The contents of this atlas are believed to be correct at the time of the latest revision. However, the publishers cannot be held responsible or liable for any loss or damage occasioned to any person acting or refraining from action as a result of any use or reliance on any material in this atlas, nor for any errors, omissions or changes in such material. This does not affect your statutory rights. The publishers would welcome information to correct any errors or omissions and to keep this atlas up to date. Please write to Publishing, The Automobile Association, Fanum House (FH12), Basing View, Basingstoke, Hampshire, RG21 4EA. E-mail: *streetbystreet@theaa.com*

Ref: ML143z

Key to map pages	ii-iii
Key to map symbols	iv-1
Enlarged map pages	2-3
Main map pages	4-53
Index – towns & villages	54
Index – streets	55-64
Index – featured places	64-65
Acknowledgements	65

Hessett

BURY ST EDMUNDS

DISS

TL TM

A14

Saxham Street

Stowupland

A140

Harleston

Stonham Aspal

A1120

Maypole Green

Rattlesden

4

49

5

Creeting St Mary

Crowfield

Bradfield St Clare

Buxhall

Stowmarket

50

Felsham

Hightown Green

Combs

6

7

Beacon Hill

Gosbeck

B1113

Needham Market

51

Coddenham

Great Green

Thorpe Green

Brettenham

Battisford Tye

Barking

B1078

B1115

Lower Street

Henl

A1141

Thorpe Morieux

Cross Green

Charles Tye

Barking Tye

B1078

Hitcham

Nedging Tye

Great Bricett

Offton

Great Blakenham

52

Claydon

Akenh

Kettlebaston

Bildeston

Naughton

Somersham

10

11

A14

Lavenham

B1078

Flowton

53

17

1

Brent Eleigh

Monks Eleigh

Ash Street

Semer

Whatfield

Elmsett

16

Bramford

Castle Hill

B1067

Swingleton Green

B1115

Milden

B1115

Aldham

Sproughton

54

22

23

2

Little Waldingfield

Lindsey

Kersey

28

A1071

29

Hintlesham

A1214

Great Waldingfield

Wicker Street Green

Hadleigh

Duke Street

Washbrook

55

Chantry

2

Groton

Boxford

Layham

B1070

30

Belstead

31

56

Newton

A1071

Raydon

Little Wenham

32

A12

Wherstead

3

Assington

A134

B1068

Polstead

38

39

A137

Tattingston White Hor

SUDBURY

Leavenheath

Stoke-by-Nayland

Holton St Mary

Capel St Mary

Bentley

48

Holb

Honey Tye

Higham

31

44

45

46

47

B1080

Stutt

B1087

Nayland

Thorington Street

B1068

30

East Bergholt

B1070

Brantham

Bures

Wissington

B1029

Cattawade

Rive

Wormingford

Boxted Cross

Manningtree

Mistley

Bradfie

A134

Langham

Lawford

B1508

Great Horkesley

TL TM

COLCHESTER

Ardleigh

Bradfield Heath

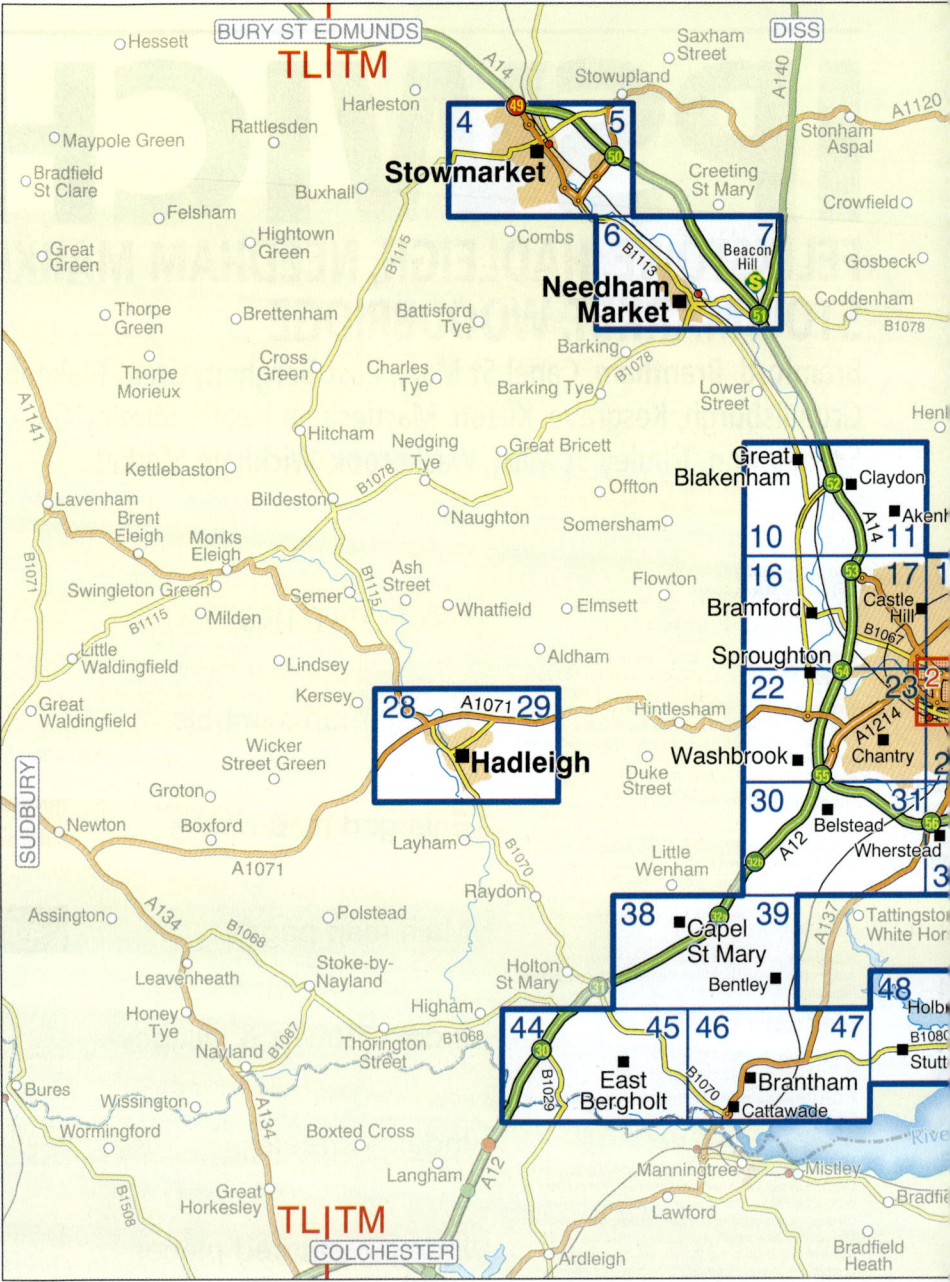

Scale of enlarged map pages 1:10,000 6.3 inches to 1 mile

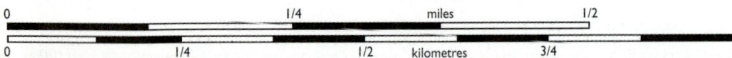

0   1/4   miles   1/2

0   1/4   1/2   kilometres   3/4   1

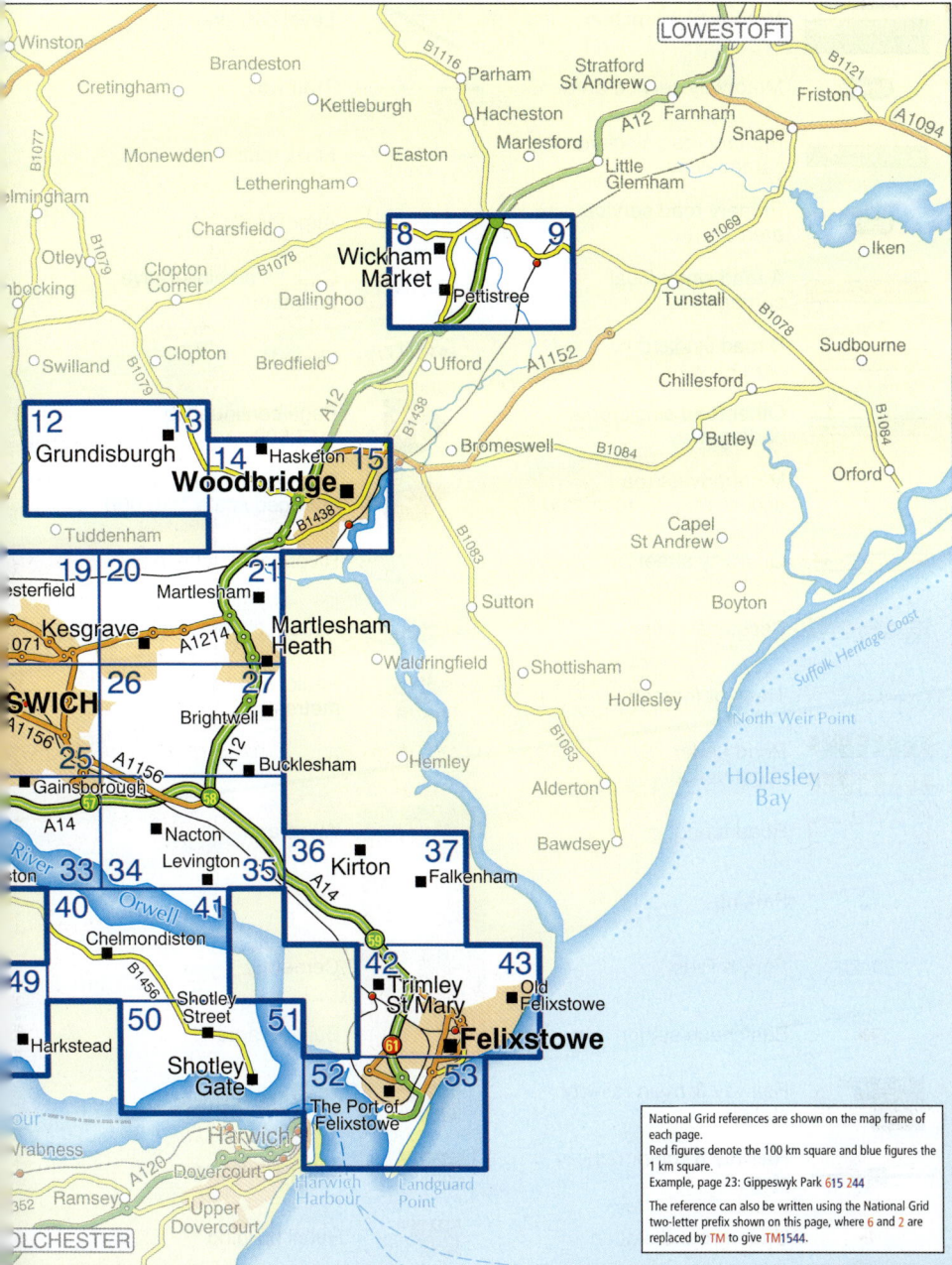

National Grid references are shown on the map frame of each page.
Red figures denote the 100 km square and blue figures the 1 km square.
Example: page 23: Gippeswyk Park 615 244

The reference can also be written using the National Grid two-letter prefix shown on this page, where 6 and 2 are replaced by TM to give TM1544.

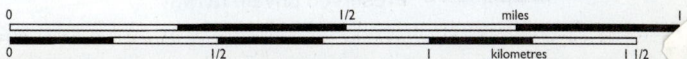

3.6 inches to 1 mile — Scale of main map pages — 1:17,500

iv

Junction 9	Motorway & junction	*LC*	Level crossing
Services	Motorway service area		Tramway
	Primary road single/dual carriageway		Ferry route
Services	Primary road service area		Airport runway
	A road single/dual carriageway		County, administrative boundary
	B road single/dual carriageway		Mounds
	Other road single/dual carriageway	17	Page continuation 1:17,500
	Minor/private road, access may be restricted	3	Page continuation to enlarged scale 1:10,000
	One-way street		River/canal, lake, pier
	Pedestrian area		Aqueduct, lock, weir
	Track or footpath	465 Winter Hill ▲	Peak (with height in metres)
	Road under construction		Beach
	Road tunnel		Woodland
P	Parking		Park
P+	Park & Ride		Cemetery
	Bus/coach station		Built-up area
	Railway & main railway station		Industrial building
	Railway & minor railway station		Leisure building
⊖	Underground station		Retail building
⊖	Light railway & station		Other building
	Preserved private railway		

ᴖᴖᴖᴖᴖᴖᴖ	City wall	♜	Castle	
A&E	Hospital with 24-hour A&E department	🏛	Historic house or building	
PO	Post Office	Wakehurst Place NT	National Trust property	
📖	Public library	Ⓜ	Museum or art gallery	
i	Tourist Information Centre	♞	Roman antiquity	
i	Seasonal Tourist Information Centre	⚊	Ancient site, battlefield or monument	
⬛🟥	Petrol station, 24 hour Major suppliers only	🏭	Industrial interest	
†	Church/chapel	❀	Garden	
🚻	Public toilets	⊚	Garden Centre Garden Centre Association Member	
♿	Toilet with disabled facilities	🌷	Garden Centre Wyevale Garden Centre	
PH	Public house AA recommended	♣	Arboretum	
🍴	Restaurant AA inspected	🛒	Farm or animal centre	
Madeira Hotel	Hotel AA inspected	🦌	Zoological or wildlife collection	
🎭	Theatre or performing arts centre	🦜	Bird collection	
📽	Cinema	🐋	Nature reserve	
⚑	Golf course	🐟	Aquarium	
▲	Camping AA inspected	**V**	Visitor or heritage centre	
🚐	Caravan site AA inspected	♈	Country park	
▲🚐	Camping & caravan site AA inspected	⌒	Cave	
🎡	Theme park	�ֹ	Windmill	
🏚	Abbey, cathedral or priory	🍶	Distillery, brewery or vineyard	

18

Christch Park

School
Ipswich School

CHEVALLIER ST
A1214
ROAD
NORWICH ROAD
Bramford Road
Waterloo Road
Providence Lane
Wellington St

Anglesea Road
Bowthorpe
Ivry
Warrington
Holly Rd
Henley
Way

Anglesea Road
Surgery
Ipswich School
Pre-Prep Dept

B1067
Sirdar Road
Gatacre Road
Beaufort St
Prospect Rd
Mountbatten Court
Opford
Rendlesham Rd
Bulwer Road

Cumberland
Cardigan Street
Alpe Street
Ann St
south st
Orford
Redan
Geneva Road
Berners St
Cecil St
Dykes St
High St
George's St
Charles St
Fitzroy
Claude St
William

The Suffolk Nuffield
Hospital at
Christchurch Park

Handford Hall
Primary School

A1214 YARMOUTH ROAD
Suffolk
Retail Park

Surrey Road
Prospect
Street
Victoria Street
London Road

Ainslie Road
Bulwer Road
Barrack La
BBC
Radio Suffolk
ST MATTHEW'S STREET

Ipswich
Museum
Crown Pools

Sikh
Temple

A137 WEST END ROAD

Elliott Street
Dillwyn Street
Emlen St
Dillwyn
Burlington Rd
Dalton Road
Portman Rd
Crescent Rd
Surgery
St Matthew's
CE Primary
School

Wolsey
Theatre
A1022 CIVIC DR

A1156 CROWN ST
Tower Ramparts
Westgate St
Cornhill
Providence St
Twr Ramparts
Shop Cen
PO
County Town Hall
Corn
Exchange
Tavern
The
Walk

Portmans Wk
Ind Centre

Aldenham Road
Firmin St
Canham St
Gt Gipping St
Little Gipping St
Portman Road

A1022 CIVIC DRIVE
Police
Stn
Black Horse La
Magistrates
Court
Willis
Corroon Bldg
FRANCISCAN WY
Curriers'
Chalon St
Cardinal St
Friars St
Falcon St
King St
Buttermarket
Ancient House

Buttermarket
Shop Centre

Bibb Way

Sir Alf Ramsey Way
Bus
Depot
Ipswich Town FC
(Portman Road)
Constantine Road
Council Building
Friars Br Rd
Greyfriars

New Cardinal St
Princes Street
Cecilia St
Wolsey St
Grey Friars Rd
Cutler St
Rose Lane
St Peter's St
Turret La
Novotel
Old Cattle
Market

23 END
Russell Road
Crown Ct
Cineworld
Cardinal
Retail Park

STAR
COLLEGE S

5 Ret Pa
Works
CHANCERY RD
Fire
Station
Royal Mail
Sorting Office
A137
GRAFTON WY
WEST END RD
GRAFTON WAY A137
Works

BRIDGE ST
A137

Gippeswyk
Park
6
B1075
A137
COMMERCIAL RD
Retail Park
Gipping Valley River Path
River Orwell
Stoke
Bridge

PRINCES ST
B1073 BURRELL ROAD
Station Yd

Gippeswyk Av
Gippeswyk
Road
Ipswich
Station
Ancaster Rd
Willoughby
Road
Chesham
Road
Belstead Road
Selwyn Cl
Seymour
Road

7
Birkfield Cl
Birkfield Drive
Kesteven Road
Grantham
Road
Philip Road
Luther Road
Martin Rd
Rectory Road
Little's Crs
Ashley St
Shelley St
Bradley St
Hartley St
Kenyon
St

24
Stoke
616
Belstead Avenue
Croft St

1 grid square represents 250 metres

F G H 18 J K

IP4

WESTERFIELD B1077

WOODBRIDGE I

Parkside Avenue
Tuddenham Road
Vermont Road
Vermont Crs
Bransby Gdns
Belvedere Road
Lonsdale Cl
Hutland Road
Allington Close
Stuart Close
Parade Rd
Rivers St
Khartoum Road
Lombard Ct
Boston Road

ALBION HILL
St Mary's Catholic Primary School
St Anthonys Crs
Burnham Close
Cauldwell Av
Holland Rd
Tovell's Rd

Christchurch
Withipoll Street
St Margarets CE Primary School
Hervey Street
Suffolk Road
Hayhill Road
Tuddenham Av
Norfolk Road
Cemetery
Fincley Road
Bank Rd
Bank Rd
North Hill
North Rd
North Hill Gdns
Post Mill Close
St Marys Rd
Oakstea Clos
Trafalgar Close

2

BOLTON LANE
Cobbold Ms
PO
Samuel Court
Blanche St
Arthurs Terrace
WOODBRIDGE ROAD
A1071
Upton Cl
Warwick Road
Nottidge Street
Belle Vue Road
Ashmere Grove
Alexandra Road
Brtnlmw Street
Spring Road
Spring Road
Masons Cl
Tokio Rd
Weymouth Road

3

St Margaret's St
Cobbold St
DOANE ST
B1077
Old Foundry Rd
Regent Thtr
Surgery
A1156
Cobden Place
St Clench
Sk St
Newton Rd
St Helens Primary Sch
Jefferies Road
Palmerston Road
Lacey Street
Lancaster Road
Wells
Belle Vue Road

astgate hop Cen
ST HELEN'S ST
ARGYLE
ST HELEN'S ST
County Hall
Register-Office
A1156
Dene
Rope
Regent St
Milner St
Oxford Road
Grange Rd
B1075
GROVE LANE
Finbars Walk
Clifford Rd
Clifford Rd Primary Sch
Tennyson Road
Darwin Roa
Faraday Rd

4

Cox La
Upr Barclay St
Orwell St
BOND STREET
Rope Wk
Kings Avenue
Woodville Road
Melville Rd
Rosebery Road
Wellesley Road
Ruskin Road

Blackfriars Priory Hall
& Smarts ses
WATERWORKS STREET
Suffolk College of HE & FE
Alexandra Park
Hill House Road
Foxhall Road
B1075

24

STAR LA
GRIMWADE ST
New St
Long St
Back Hamlet
Devonshire Road
Gladstone Road
Cavendish Street
Up

5

PO
Fore St Pool
Salvation Army
FORE STREET A1156
Works
White Elm St
Mitre Way
The Beeches
Nacton Road
Rosehill Road
Alston Road
Alan Road

6

A1022
Neptune Quay
Wherry Quay
Neptune Quay
Salthouse Harbour Hotel
Old Custom's House
Coprolite Street
FORE HAMLET
BISHOP'S HILL
Plough Street
Pownall Rd
Unity St
Rose's Crs
Sandhurst Avenue
A1156
FE
Rose

IPSWICH
Marina
Neptune Quay
DUKE STREET
B1458
Wykes Bishop St
Maude St
Anchor St
Patteson Rd
John St
Myrtle Rd
Holwells Cl
Trinity St
Works
Holywells Park

West Dock
Stoke
Suffolk Coast & Heaths Path
Felaw Street
Mather Way
Purplett St
HAWES ST
Helena Road
CLIFF ROAD B1458
Holy We
Ship Launch Road

7

F 5th Street G H 24 J K IP3

Works
Suffolk Coast & Heaths Path
Beech Gro
Nacton Road
Elmhurst Drive

4

Onehouse

Woodside Farm

Eden House

Spike's La

BURY ROAD

NEWTON ROAD

B1113

Shepher

6 03 04

A B C D E

Northfield Road

Birch Rd

Road

Lower Road

Littlesden River

B1115

FINBOROUGH ROAD

Combs Lane

Starhouse Lane

Union Road

Wash La

Fen Farm

Boyton Hall

Combs Lane

Valley Farm

STOWMARKET

Shakespeare Rd

Lngfrd Lngfrd Cl
Mcfld Rd
Beckett's
Kipling Way
Shron Cl
Okeral
Ct
Priestly Cl
Purcell
Cl
Walton
Holst Rd
Hall Road
Britten Av
Holst Md

Spencer Way
Lowry Way
Blake
Tr
Rd

Wood Ley Community School

Mid Suffolk Leisure Centre

Stowmarket High School

Chilton Way

Brook
Cristbl
Wy

St Edmunds

Chilton Community Prim Sch

Cemy

St Edmunds

Cherry Tree Rd

Gowle Rd

A14

A14

J49

A1398

The Oslers

BURY RD

Crown

Beech Ter

Pound Lane

Gainsborough

St Mary's Rd

Kingsmead Close

PO

Kent Rd

Violet

Soames Cl

Grebe
Ct
Heron Cl
Mallard
Dr
Drake
Cl
Swan
Cl

Ridgeway
Winchester
Thirlmere
Treeview
Drive

Boulters
Cl

Onehouse

Chilton Av

St Peter's Rd
Windermere Rd
Elm Rd

Stowmarket Middle School

Curwen Rd

Page's

Recreation Road

Childe Rd

Fairfield

Hill

Thurlow

Bury
St

Tavern
St

TAVERN STN

Crows Rd

Rydal

Town
Gn

West View
Beaumont Wy

Danescourt Av

Millfield

Underhill

Viking Rd
Seabreeze

Abbots Hall Prim Sch

Lucena Ct

The
Brickfields

Illiffe Way

Crow La

Crow

Museum of East Anglian Life

Abbot's Hall

Temple

LOC

Ockington

Crs

Camplon
Crs

Baldwin Rd
Orwell Rd
Aldis Av

Edgecomb Road

Jubilee Avenue

Edgar

Farrier's
Rd
Millers
Cl

The Ts

Normandy

Rise

Hunt
Cl

Wright
Cl

Church

Combs Wd Dr

Road

Poplar Hill

Model Farm

Jack

's Lane

1 grid square represents 500 metres

60 59 58 57

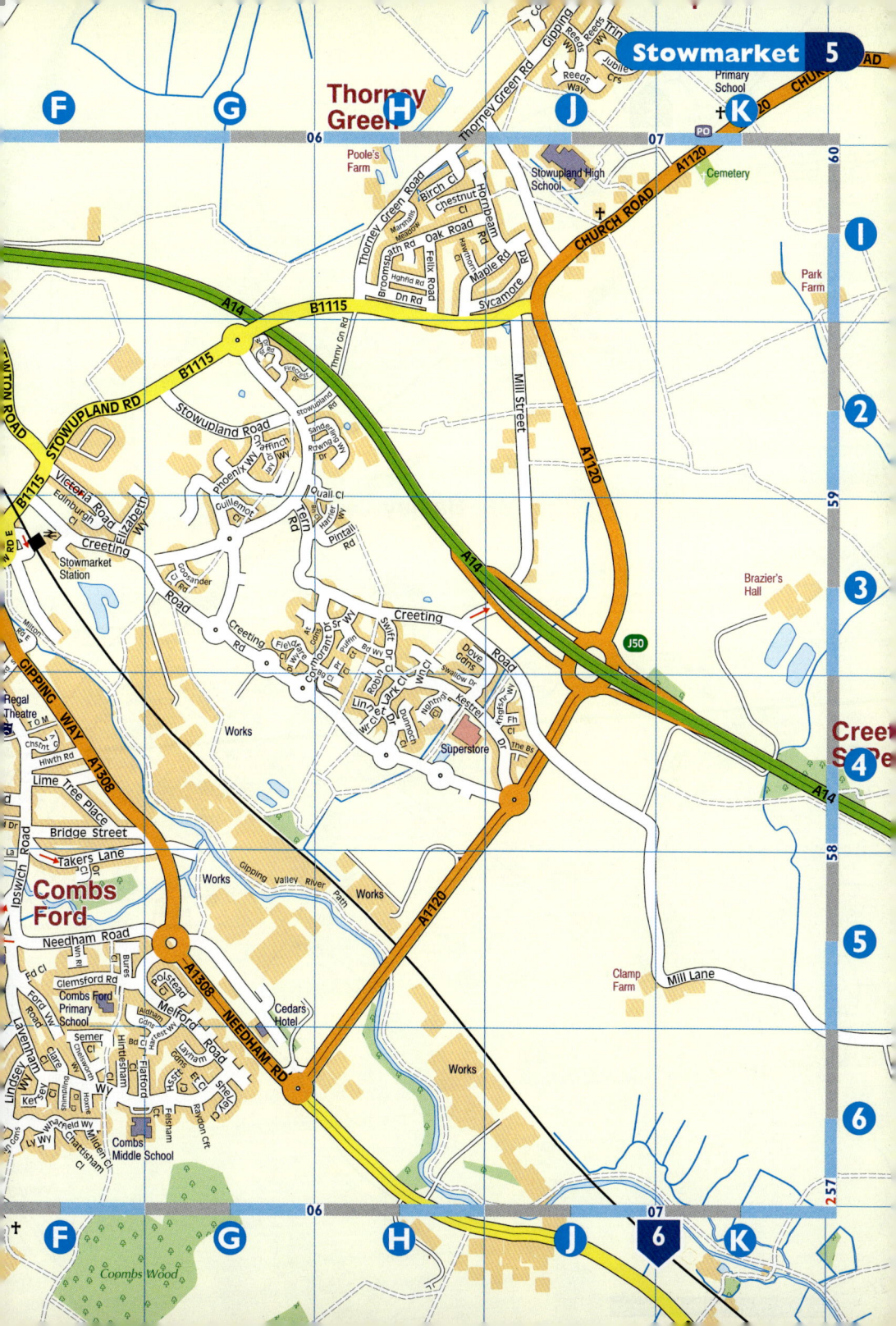

Thorney Green

Thorney Green Rd

Gipping Wy
Reeds Wy
Reeds
Trin
Jubile
Crs

Primary School

† K

PO

CHUR RD

A1120

CHURCH ROAD

Cemetery

Poole's Farm

Thorney Green Road

Birch Cl
Chestnut Cl
Hornbeam
Oak Road
Maple Rd
Sycamore
Felix Road
Hghfld Rd
Dn Rd
Broomspath Rd
Marigold

Stowupland High School

†

Park Farm

I

Mill Street

A14

B1115

A14

Stowupland Road

Stowupland Rd

B1115

STOWUPLAND RD

B1115

2

59

60

Tmmy On Rd

Phoenix Wy
Guillemot
Fern Rd
Quail Cl
Pintail Rd

Affinch

Sanders
Rowing Dr

3

Brazier's Hall

Victoria Road
Edinburgh Cl
Elizabeth Wy

Creeting Station
Stowmarket Station

Gosander Cl

Creeting Rd
Fieldfare
Cormorant Dr
Swift Dr
Creeting
Puffin Rd
Dove Gdns
Swallow Dr
Lark Cl
Wn Cl
Kestrel
Linn
Dunnoc
Highthpl
Fh Cl
The Bs

Creeting Road

J50

Creet
S

4

58

Regal Theatre

Gipping Wy
A1308

Lime Tree Place

Bridge Street

Takers Lane

Combs Ford

Works

Superstore

A1120

Works

Gipping Valley River Path

Works

Clamp Farm

Mill Lane

5

A14

Needham Road

Glemsford Rd
Combs Ford Primary School
Polstead
Melford Road
A1308
NEEDHAM RD

Cedars Hotel

Lindsey Wy
Lavenham
Clare
Kersey Cl
Semer
Chelsworth Cl
Hintlesham
Flatford
Gynam
Felsham
Combs Middle School
Chattisham
Raydon Cft

Works

6

57

Coombs Wood

6

A **5** **B** **C** **D** **E**
6 07 08

Works

Mill L...

Hill Farm

I

Creeting Hall

Grove Farm

Mill Lane

57

STOWMARKET

River Path

Gipping Valley

Jack's

2

Badley WK

ROAD

River Gipping

Watering Farm

B1113

56

BADLEY HILL

Gipping Valley River Path

Badley Hill

STOWMARKET ROAD

LC

3

Hill House Farm

Hill House Lane

Gipsy La

Ethld Rd

B1113 Road

Meadow rw.

Skeggall Cl

pagel Cl

Ludbrook

Ludbrook

Orchard Ga

Anderson La

Anderson

Ludbrook

Hawks Mill St

LC

Mill St

Cl

n Swn

Hurstlea

Council Building

4

55

Platten

Burton Dr

Alexander Cl

Gilbert Cl

Bridge St

PO

The

Barrett's

Crowley Rd

Priestly Rd

Am

Rd

Theobald

Park Road

The Causeway

School J

HIGH S

5

Lane

Cem

Quinton

Bosmere Primary School

Quinton Road

Needham Market Middle School

Morris Wy

ckson Cl

Chainhouse

Alcorn Wy

Hargrave

6

254

Gibbon's Farm

Lupin Wy

Primrose

Clover Cl

Orchd Wy

Lilac Wk

Foxglove

Cwslp Wy

Rose Wy

Bell Cl

Avenue

Surgery

A **B** **C** **D** **E**
6 07 seway 08

Hascot

I grid square represents 500 metres

F G H J K

Creeting St Mary

I

Creeting St Mary Primary School

All Saints Road

Church Lane

St Mary's Gdns

A14

A140

Holt's Lane

Holt's Lane

Buck's Head La

Codde Gre

Flordon Road

edham rket

Sally

Wood's

Lane

Needham Market Station

Gipping Valley River Path

Works

B1078

Flordon Road

CODDENHAM RD

Coddenham Road

A14

Hungercut Hall

Needham Lake

CODDENHAM ROAD

LC

A140

KETTLE LANE

Bosmere Hall

Travelodge

Pinecroft Wy

Lion La

Lion Barn Industrial Est

Maitland Rd

Williamsport Wy

Gipping Valley River Path

Norwich Road

Long Covert

J51

Grinstead Hill

LOWER STREET B1113

LOWER STREE

F G H J K

Pipps Ford

57 56 55 254

A   B   C   D   E

6 29   30   Easton   Road

57

Easton Road

Glevering
Hall Farm

River Deben

I

Valley
Farm

Glevering
Bridge

B1078

B1078

N

HIGH ST   LOWER ST

As

The Drift   Riverside VW

2

Potsford
Wood

BORDER COT LA

HIGH ST

56

Gelham
Hall

Simon's Cross

Broad Rd

Churchill Crs

Pkwy

Barnhams
Way

Kg Edward Av

Spring Lane

Broadway

Churchill
Cl

Wickham
Community
Primary School

Broad Road

Yew Tree Rd

Meadowside

3

Dallinghoo Road

Orchard Pl

Elm Rd

Line Rd

Dallinghoo Rd

Crown La

Church Ter

Birch Cl

The Crs

Willow
Tree Cl

PO

Mill   Lane

B145

Dallinghoo Road

Thong
Hall

Vinery
Cl

Whincroft

Simoy La

Green Lane

4

Thong Hall Road

Cemetery

Chapel   Lane

55

Grove Road

Grove
Farm

Walnuts Lane

Rogue's La

5

Grove Road

Home
Farm

The   Street

B1438

Loudham   Hall   Road

Pettistree

Green
Farm

Presmere Road

Loudham
Hall

6

Byng Lane

Stump St

Java

Lodge Rd

Pettistree
House

Low
Farm

2 54

Byng Lane

Byng Brook

B1438

Ufford   Road

6 29   30   A12

A12

A   B   C   D   E

Byng

Byng
Hall

A12   PD B1438

I grid square represents 500 metres

River

F G H J K

MAIN ROAD

A12

B1078

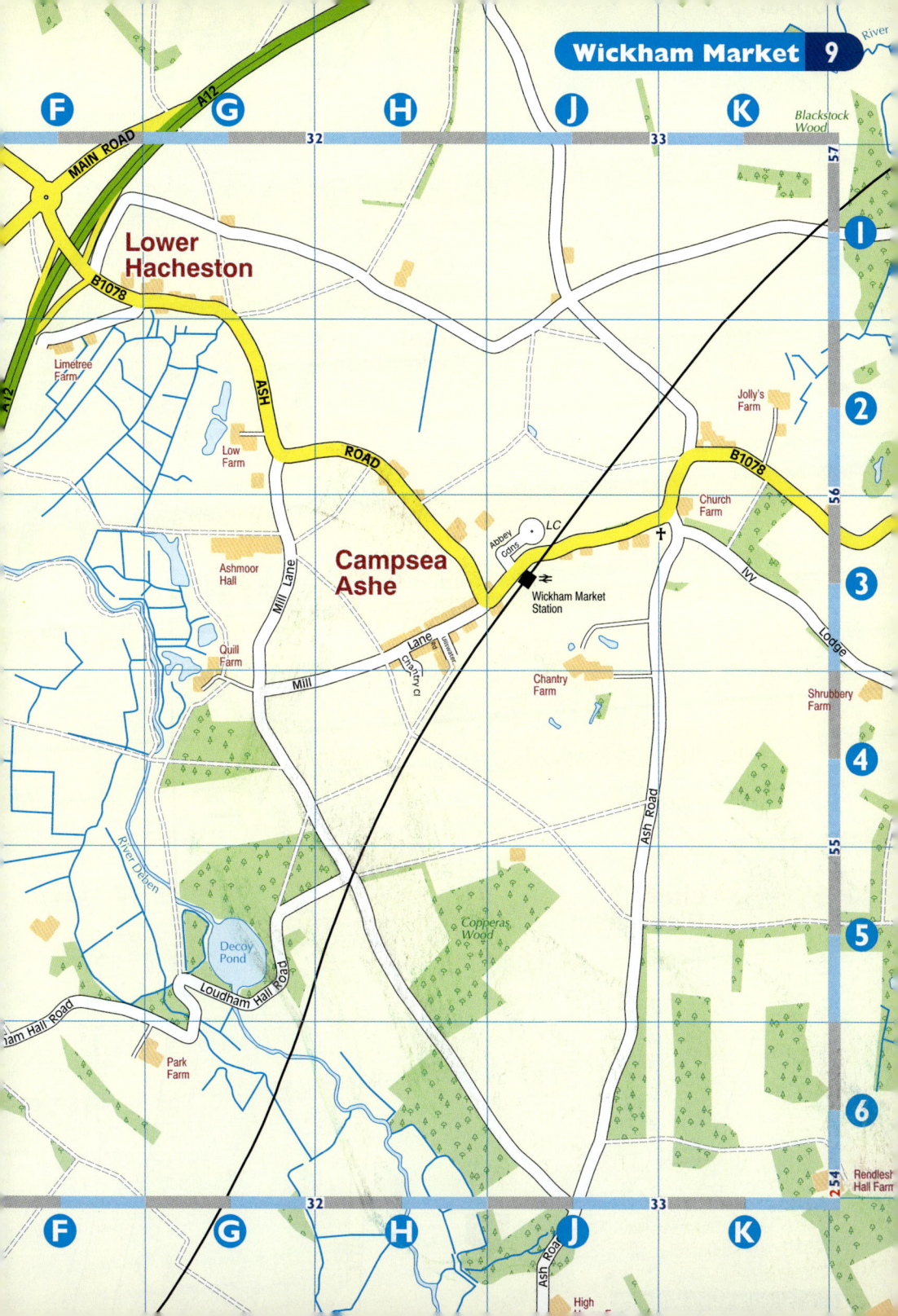

**Lower
Hacheston**

Limetree
Farm

ASH

Low
Farm

ROAD

Ashmoor
Hall

Mill Lane

**Campsea
Ashe**

Quill
Farm

MILL

Chantry Cl

Lane

Abbey
Gdns

LC

Wickham Market
Station

Chantry
Farm

Blackstock
Wood

I

Jolly's
Farm

2

B1078

56

Church
Farm

IVY

3

Lodge

Shrubbery
Farm

4

55

River Deben

Decoy
Pond

Loudham Hall Road

Copperas
Wood

Ash Road

5

...ham Hall Road

Park
Farm

6

2 54

Rendlesh...
Hall Farm

F G H J K

High

32 33

A B C D E

51

I

Chalk Hill

Chequers Rise

Kingfisher Dr

Mill Lane

Mill Lane

Cem

Hood Dr

Wnyt Gdns

Keytes Way

Hood Dr

Stowmarket Rd

Aston

B1113

Claremen

Plummers Dell

Claydon Business Park

Gipping Valley River Path

Works

Lower Pesthouse Lane

The Crescent

The Crescent

Norwich Road

Great Blakenham

Claydon Business Park

Bridge Trading Estate

Gipping

LC

Road

Works

Masc Ct

Fitchr

Coopers

First W

St Pe

Static

2

50

Column Field Quarry

Works

Barn

Blue

La

Chapel

Lane

Addison Way

New Industrial Site

Lodge

Council Building

Lane

Works

3

Cottage Farm

Blackacre Hill

On On Av

Bramford Road

J52

4

49

Broomvale Farm

The Common

Broomvale Business Centre

River Gipping

The Beeches

Little Blakenham

Road

Somersham Road

Pound Lane

Bramford Road B1113

5

6

Suffolk Water Park

Paper Mill Lane

2 48

A B C D E

611 12

16

Stowmarket Road

Bramford Road

Sycamore Farm

The Common

Somers

Works

Works

Henl

F

G IP6

H **Barham**

J

K

Cooper's

Church Lane

Manor Farm

51

I

Rede Woods

Rede L

Claydon

Church Lane

Old Rectory Cl

Phillipps Rd

Eddowes Rd

Woodlea Gardens

Glebe

Manor Rd

Ely Rd

Lincoln Gdns

Beacon Road

Thornhill Road

Balcon Rd

York Road

Jubilee Close

Edinburgh Gardens

Lancaster Way

Exeter Rd

High House Farm

Rede Lane

2

50

Claydon Primary School

Claydon High School

The Slade

Highfield Dr

Church Lane

Church Lane

Church Lane

The Knole

Church Lane

Church Lane

The Knole

Crescent

Back Lane

Drift

Country

Morgan Ct

Newell Rise

The Beeches

Church Lane

PO

Poplar Cl

Chestnut Dr

Laurel Wy

Tree Cl

Rowan Cl

Aspen Close

Elm Cl

Hazel Rise

Willow Cl

Hall La

3

Orchard

Old La

Ipswich Road

Old La

Ipswich Road

4

Bower Farm

Works

Hill View Business Park

49

Mockbeggars Hall

Rise Hall

Akenham

5

Old Norwich Road

Thurleston Lane

6

2 48

F

G

H

17

J

K

J53

BUR

lands Way

Anglia Pkwy

P+

Old

Thurleston High School

Carlyle Cl

Carlyle Cl

Mitford Close

Epsom

Thurleston Church Lane

Primary
School

B1077

A **B** **C** **D** **E**

52 | 619 | 20

1

Newton
Hall

Clopton Road

2

Whitehouse
Farm

Laurel
Farm

Wash Lane

Clopton Road

3

MOW HILL

Burw

Sycamore
Farm

Clopton
Road

Wood
Farm

4

Redhouse
Farm

Bull Hall Lane

Sandy
Lane

Sandy
Street

5

Hillbrow
Farm

Clopton Road

Culpho
Wood

Valley
Farm

iggle

50

6

Witnesham
La

Abbey
Farm

Cu

Tuddenham
Hall

2 49 | 619 | 20

A **B** **C** **D** **E**

Clopton Road

Grundisburgh Road

Culpho
Hall

1 grid square represents 500 metres

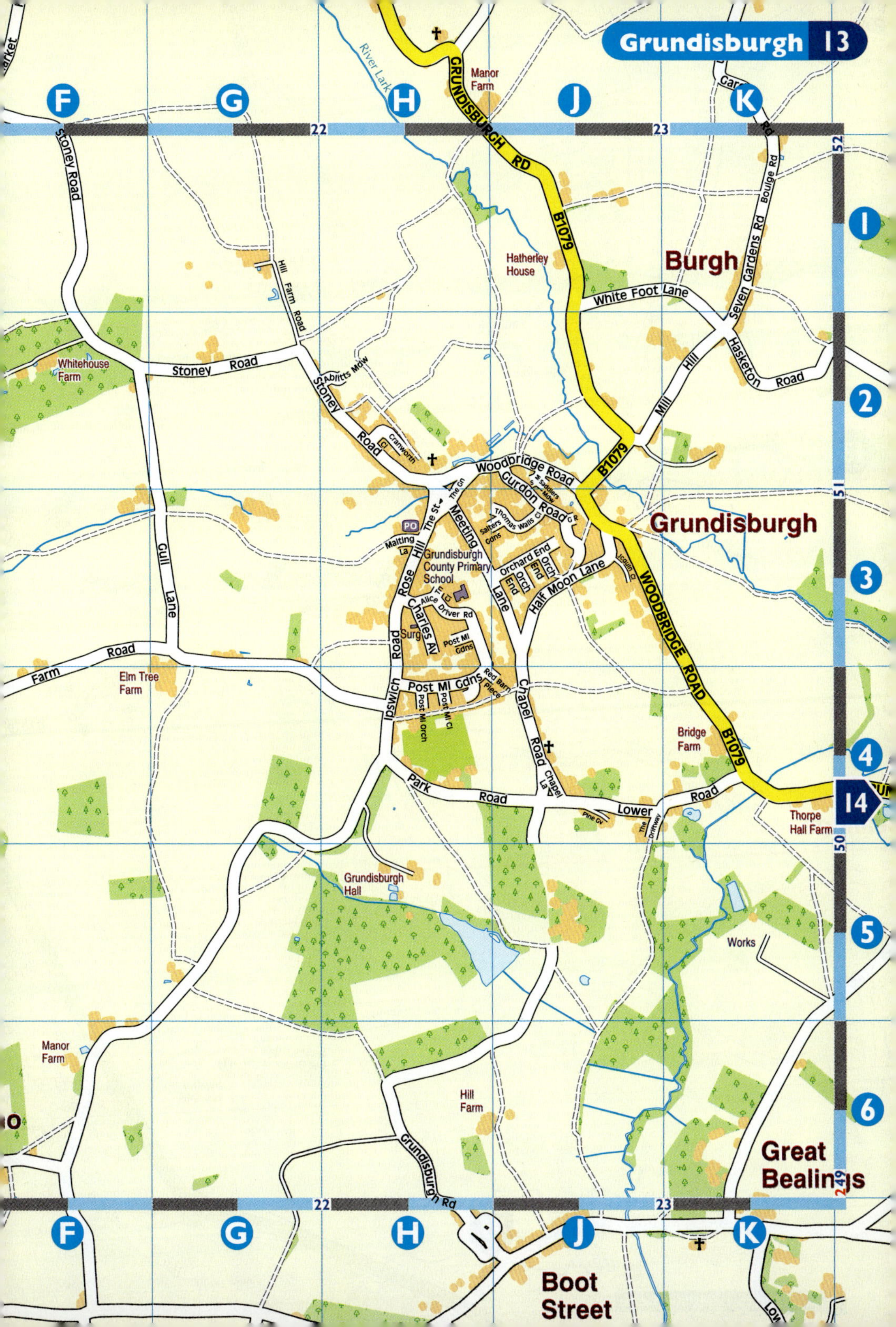

F
G
H
J
K

River Lark

Manor Farm

GRUNDISBURGH RD

B1079

22

23

52

I

Burgh

Hatherley House

White Foot Lane

Seven Gardens Rd

Garden Rd

Bouge Rd

Hasketon Road

Hill

Mill

2

51

Whitehouse Farm

Stoney Road

Stoney Road

Hill Farm Road

Stoney Road

Ditts Mdw

Cranmoth

Woodbridge Road

Curdon Road

Grundisburgh

3

Gull Lane

Rose Hill

Meeting La

The St

The Ln

PO

Malting La

Salters Gdns

Thomas Walls

Orchard End Orch End

Orch End

Half Moon Lane

WOODBRIDGE ROAD

B1079

Grundisburgh County Primary School

Alice Driver Rd

Surg

Charles Av

Post MI Gdns

Post MI Orch

Post MI Gdns

Post MI Cl

Red Barn

Pine Cl

Chapel Road

Chapel La

Bridge Farm

4

Farm Road

Elm Tree Farm

Ipswich Road

Park Road

Lower Road

Pine Cv

The Driveway

Road

14

50

Thorpe Hall Farm

Grundisburgh Hall

5

Works

Manor Farm

Hill Farm

Grundisburgh Rd

6

Great Bealings

F
G
H
J
K

22

23

249

Grundisburgh Rd

LOW

Boot Street

A **B** **C** **D** **E**

6 24 25

I

51

Watery La

Works

IP13

Boulge Road

Low Road
Top Rd

Hasketon

Home Farm

Tymmes Pl

Blacksmiths Road

Church Road

Church Farm

Riverside

Mill Lane

2

13

Ha...

50

GRUNDISBURGH RD

Pinners Lane

Shrubbery Road

B1079

Bealings Lane

GRUNDISBURGH ROAD

Hasketon Grange

Yew Tree House

Shrubbery Road

Manor

Blacksmiths Rd Road

3

GRUNDISBURGH RD

Works

Wyevale Garden Centre

B1079

4

49

Great Bealings

Rosery Lane

Bealings House

Seckford Hall

5

PO

...ver St

Lodge Road

Rosery Farm

Seckford Golf Centre

St Peter's Cl

St Annes Cl

Oxford Drive

Christchurch Drive

Seckford Hall Rd

Seckford Hall Hotel

Peterhou...

Gittor...

Grays

Magdale...

6

48

Golf Course

A12

Fynn Rd

Clayton Ct

Crane Cl

IPSWICH

2

6 24 25

Fynn Valley Walk

A **B** **21** **C** **D** **E**

A12

B1438

Top St

Brock La...

...Valley Walk

1 grid square represents 500 metres

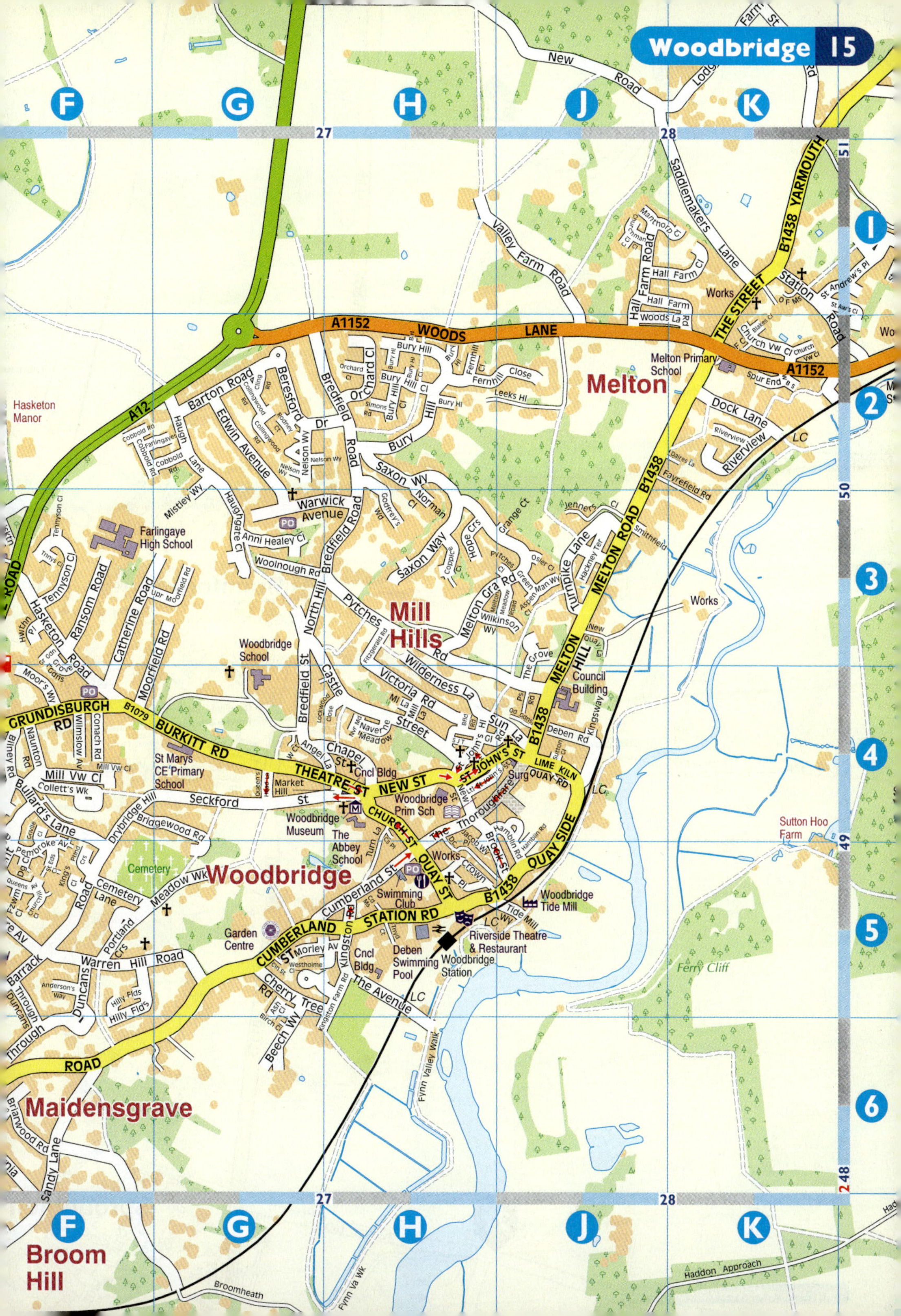

F
G
H
J
K
27
28
New Road
Lodge
A12
A1152 WOODS LANE
A1152
Valley Farm Road
Saddlemakers Lane
B1438 YARMOUTH
THE STREET
Station Road
Hall Farm Road
Hall Farm Cl
Hall Farm
Woods La Rd
Works
Church Vw Cl
Melton Primary School
Melton
Spur End
Dock Lane
Riverview
LC
Fayrefield Rd
Hasketon Manor
Barton Road
Beresford
Bredfield Road
Orchard Cl
Bury Hill
Bury Hill Cl
Fernhill Cl
Fernhill Close
Leeks Hl
Haugh Lane
Edwin Avenue
Nelson Wy
Dr
Saxon Wy
Norman Cl
Warwick Avenue
Mistley Wy
Haughgate Cl
Anni Healey Cl
Woolnough Rd
Farlingaye High School
Tennyson Cl
Hasketon Road
Ransom Road
Catherine Road
Moorfield Rd
North Hill
Pytches Rd
Saxon Way
Hope Crs
Grange Ct
Jennet's Cl
Smithfield
Turnpike Lane
Hackney Ter
MELTON ROAD B1438
Mill Hills
Melton Gra Rd
Wilkinson Wy
Works
New Quay La
The Grove
MELTON HILL
Council Building
Wilderness La
Victoria Rd
Woodbridge School
Castle Street
Bredfield St
Sun La
Deben Rd
Kingsway
GRUNDISBURGH RD
B1079
BURKITT RD
Moor's Wy
Conach Rd
Wilmslow Av
Mill Vw Cl
Naunton Rd
Chapel St
Cncl Bldg
THEATRE ST
NEW ST
ST JOHN'S ST
B1438
LIME KILN QUAY RD
Surg
St Marys CE Primary School
Market Hill
Seckford St
Collett's Wk
Bullard's Lane
Drybridge Hill
Briggewood Rd
Woodbridge Museum
Woodbridge Prim Sch
The Thoroughfare
CHURCH ST
The Abbey School
Hamblin Rd
QUAY SIDE
Cemetery
Meadow Wk
Woodbridge
Works
QUAY ST
Crown Pl
Woodbridge Tide Mill
Tide Mill Wy
Cemetery Lane
Portland Crs
Cumberland St
Swimming Club
B1438
STATION RD
Riverside Theatre & Restaurant
Garden Centre
CUMBERLAND ST
Morley Av
Kingston Rd
Cncl Bldg
Deben Swimming Pool
Woodbridge Station
Warren Hill Road
Barrack
Duncans
Cherry Tree Rd
Kingston Farm Rd
The Avenue
LC
Ferry Cliff
Sutton Hoo Farm
Beech Wy
Through
ROAD
Maidensgrave
Briarwood Rd
Sandy Lane
Fynn Valley Walk
Broom Hill
Broomheath
Fynn Va Wk
Haddon Approach
51
50
49
248
1
2
3
4
5
6

A B 10 C D E

611 12

I

2

3

4

5

6

47

48

46

45

Somersham

Somersham Road

Suffolk Water Park

The Common

Works

Works

Paper Mill Lane

River Gipping

Grove H

Gipping Va River Path

B1113

LORAINE WAY

Sycamore Farm

Rutters Farm

Tye Lane

Miller's Wood

Cemetery

B1067

THE STREET

Acton Road

Acton Gdns

Flindell Dr

Chapel Field

Fraser

Mill Road

Acton Rd

Acton Close

Acton Rd

Bramford

Bullen Close

Avenue

Broke

Mill Fld

Gipping Way

Package

Leggatt Dr

Bullen Lane

Hall

Walk

Bullen Lane

ullenhall arm

Bullen Lane

Angel Rd

Orchard Road

Gipping Rd

Tinastone Rd

Ravens Lane

PO

Pr

Bramford CE Primary Sch

Duckamere

St Mary's Cl

Church cn

SHIP LANE

Mill Lane

Fidgeon's Farm

Fitzgerald Road

Vicarage Lane

Vicarage Close

Thornbush Hall

Thornbush La

Runcton Farm

LORAINE WAY

Sproughton Manor

River Gipping

Grindle Farm

The Grindle

B1113

River Gipping

Sproughton Rd

Lower St

Sproughton

A 22 B C D E

611 12

Perry Barn

Burstall Lane

Beech Close

Church Cts

Ransome Close

THE STREET

Oak GV

High St

Monks

Samford Place

Church Close

Glebe

Broomfield Common

Gipping VW

Abbey Oaks

Sproughton CE Primary

F **G** **H** **J** **K**

Whitton

White House

Westbourne

Castle Hill

Roads and labels:

Bury Rd / Bury Road
Anglia Pkwy N
Anglia Pkwy S
Old Norwich Road
Whitton Church Lane
Byron Road
Goldsmith Road
Shakespeare Road
Thackeray Road
Spenser Road
Chaucer Rd
Macaulay Road
Parnell Close
Thurleston High School
Carlyle
Homer Close
Defoe Road
Maycroft
Sandown Road
Shenstone Drive
Heathercroft Rd
Kempton Road
Castle Hill J&I Sch
Shirley Close
Dryden Road
Congreve Road
Fircroft Road
Larcroft Rd
Rosecroft Road
Queensdale Close
Dales Road
Dales View Road
Park VW Rd
View Rd
Broom Hill Swimming Pool
Knightsdale Road
Princedale Cl
Silverdale Cl
Sherrington Road
Westwood Av
Kensington
Mornington Avenue
Brookfield Rd
Lambeth
All Saints Road
Brooks Hall Road
Graham Road
Chelmsford
Norwich Road
Chevalier St
Bramford Road / B1067
Sproughton Road
Sproughton Business Park
Farthing Road Industrial Estate
Superstore
Boss Hall Road
Business Park
Elton Park Industrial Est
Brookhouse Business Park
Hadleigh
Cromford Road
Handford Hall Primary Sch
Suffolk Retail Park
Sikh Temple
Yarmouth Road
London Road
Surrey Road
Victoria
Ainslie Road
Clarkson

White House J&I School
Westbourne High School
Marlow Road
Castle Road
Ravensfield
Shrubland Rd
Ravleigh Road
Lister Road
Kelvin Rd
Deben Rd
Westbourne Road
Cromer Road
Mumford Road
Broadmere Rd
Waveney Road
Wallace Road
Bennett Road
Shafto Road
High View Road
Bramford Lane
Galway Avenue
Agate Cl
Coral Drive
Brockley Crescent
Henniker Road
Diamond Road
Pearl Road
Coral Drive
Adair Road

Olympus Close
Works
Donegal Road
Wickloy Rd
Kildare Av
Wexford Road
Connaught Rd
Antrim Road
Maudslay Road
Daimler Rd
Bentley Rd
Crossley Gdns
Lovetofts Drive
Waterford Road
Ferry Ave
Morgan Drive

Norwich Road
Highfield Road
Chesterfield Drive
Tranmere Grove
Charlton Av
Preston Drive
Beechcroft Road
Pinecroft Road
Willowcroft Road
Elmcroft
Ashcroft
Cedarcroft
Everton Rd
Chelsea Close
Crescent
St Pancras Catholic Primary School
Stratford Road
Meredith Rd
Surgery
Burns Rd
Wrdswrth Crs
Browning Rd
Blake Road
Arnold Close
Coleridge Rd
Moore Rd
Burke Rd
Bunyan Close
Garrick Way
Macaulay Rd
Keats

Thomas Wolsey Special School
Alpha Business Park
Whitton Community Primary School
Ballater Close
Limerick Close

White House Road
Works
Cavan Road
Kerry Rd

Thurleston Lane
Whitton Lever
River Hill
A14
Bramford Road
Weaver Cl
Europa Way
Farthing Rd
Saturn Rd
Jovian Way
Callisto Court
Quenton Road
Boss Hall Rd
Baird
Crompton Road

J53
J54
Superstore
Goddard Road
Whitehouse Industrial Estate

23

18

2

Springfield Junior Sch
Springfield Inf Sch
Surbiton Road
Richmond Rd
Hampton Rd
Windsor Rd
Gipping Valley River Path
River Gipping

A **B** **C** **D** **E**

48 6 16 17

Westerfield

Thurleston Lane

Lower Road

Sandy Lane

Swan Lane

St Mary's Wy

Church

Goodwood Close

Sparrowe's Nest

1

Epsom Rd

Henley Rd

Ludlow Rd

June Rd

Taunton Close

Lamb

Henley Road

B1077

Fuller's Fld

PO

Lincoln Rd

Lincoln Close

Henley Avenue

Westerfield Business Centre

2

Hill

Jarroch

Kempton Rd

Palmcroft Road

Fircroft

Pearcroft Road

Aldercroft Road

Aldercroft Close

Birchcroft Rd

Larchcroft Road

Larchcroft Close

LC

Westerfield Station

Road

Rosecroft Road

Pilcroft St

Coralree Av

Clive Av

Henley Road

June Avenue

3

17

Dale Hall Primary School

Dale

The Grove

Henley Rd

Vere Gdns

Grove Farm

WESTERFIELD ROAD

Red House Farm

Tuddenham Road

Cemy

Queensdale Close

Dales Road

PO

Baronsdale Cl

Karen Close

Onehouse Lane

Hall

Henley Road

Valley Close

Bromeswell Road

Chelsworth Avenue

Dorset Cl

Ely Rd

4

Cheltenham Av

Cotswold Avenue

Ipswich Sports Club

Picton Avenue

Valley Road

Colchester Rd

Park Vw

Pine Rd

View Rd

ROAD A1214 **VALLEY**

Woodstone Av

The Avenue

Dale Hill Lane

Henley Road

Elsmere Rd

Kingsfield Avenue

Bildeston Gdns

Brettenham Crs

Valley Road

Borrowdale Av

Tuddenham Road

North Close

Carlton Wy

Berkeley Close

Ipswich Crematorium

Lane

New Cemetery

Somerset Road

Kingsdale

PO

Clare Road

5

Broom Hill Swimming Pool

Constitution

St Edmund's Rd

Greenways Close

Park Road

Manor Road

Corder Road

South Close

The Albany

Beverley Rd

Whitby Road

Graham Road

Paget Road

Warrington Road

Holly Road

Ipswich Prep School

Ipswich School

Bridle Way

Gainsborough Rd

Tuddenham Road

George Frost Close

Old Cemetery

Belgrave Close

Brunswick Road

Belvedere

6

Anglesea Rd

Orford St

Newson St

Cecil Rd

Ipswich School Pre-Prep Dept

Christchurch Park

B1077

Tremont Crescent

Suffolk Road

Finchley Rd

Halemere Drive

Bank Road

ALBION HL

WOODBF

Ivry St

Cardigan St

2

Nuffield Hospital

Fonnereau Way

Christchurch Street

Hervey St

Cemetery

3

A1071

St Mary's Catholic Prim Sch

IPSWICH

WOODBRIDGE RD

Hutland Rd

A ABC Radio

B Crown Pools

24 BOLTON LA

C School

Lacey Street

D

E

ST MATHEW'S ST

CROWN ST

Margarets Plain

WOODBRIDGE RD

St Helens

Wolsey St

Norwich Road

WEST END ROAD

1 grid square represents 500 metres

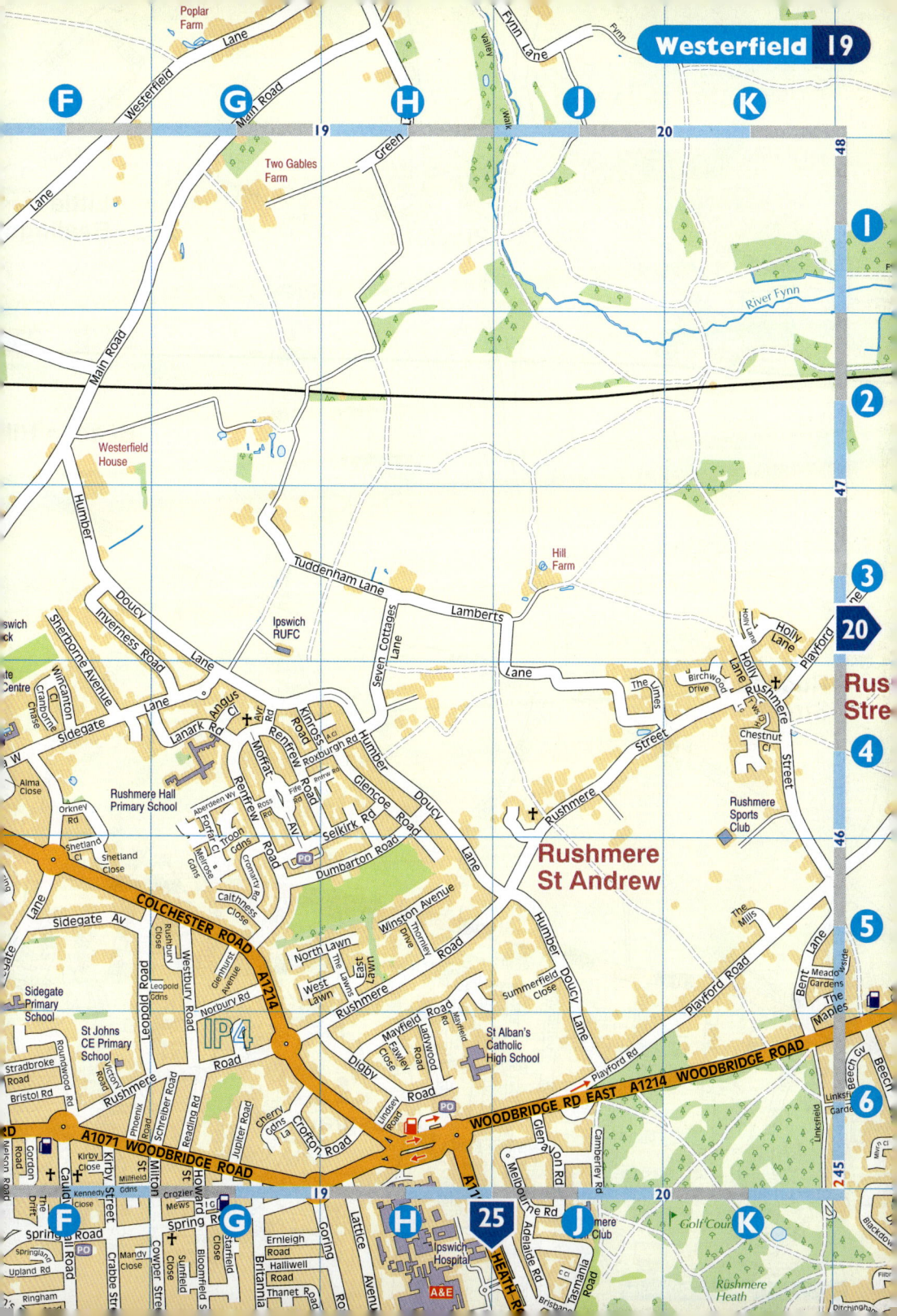

F   G   H   J   K

19   20   48

I
2
47
3
20
Rus
Stre
4
46
5
6
245

Poplar Farm
Westerfield
Lane
Main Road
Green
Fynn Lane
Valley Walk
Fynn

Two Gables Farm

River Fynn

Lane
Main Road

Westerfield House

Hill Farm

Tuddenham Lane
Lamberts
Ipswich RUFC
Seven Cottages Lane
Lane
Holly Lane
Holly Lane
Playford
Birchwood Drive
The Limes
Rushmere
Street
Chestnut Cl
Rushmere Sports Club

Doucy Lane
Sherborne Avenue
Inverness Road
Wincanton
Cranborne Chase
Sidegate Lane
Lanark Rd
Angus Cl
Renfrew Road
Kinross Rd
Roxburgh Rd
Moffat
Renfrew
Aberdeen Wy
Forfar Ave
Melrose Gdns
Troon
Ross Rd
Fife Rd
Glencoe Road
Doucy Lane
Selkirk Rd
Dumbarton Road
Caithness Close
Cromarty Rd
Humber
Rushmere
Street
The Mills

Rushmere Hall Primary School
Orkney Rd
Shetland Cl
Shetland Close
PO
Alma Close

COLCHESTER ROAD
A1214
Sidegate Av
North Lawn
West Lawn
The Lawns
Winston Avenue
Thornley Drive
Rushmere Road
Summerfield Close
Humber Doucy Lane
Playford Road
Bent Lane
The Maples
Beech Gv
Beech
Linksfield Gardens

Sidegate Primary School
Rushbury Close
Glenhurst Gdns
Westbury Road
Norbury Rd
Leopold Gdns
St Johns CE Primary School
IP4
Rushmere Road
RUSHMERE ST ANDREW
Mayfield Road
Fawley Close
Ladywood
St Alban's Catholic High School
St Alban's
Playford Rd

Stradbroke Road
Bristol Rd
Phoenix Rd
Leopold Road
Westbury Road
Victory Road
Schreiber Road
Jupiter Road
Digby
Clifton Road
Crofton Road
Lindsey Road
PO
Camberley Rd
Glenavon Rd
Melbourne Rd
Adelaide Rd
Tasmania
WOODBRIDGE RD EAST A1214 WOODBRIDGE ROAD
PLAYFORD ROAD
Golf Course

A1071 WOODBRIDGE ROAD
Gordon Rd
Kirby Close
Kennedy Close
Millford Gdns
Howard St
Crozier Mews
Spring Road
Starfield Close
Ernleigh Road
Goring Road
Lattice Avenue
Ipswich Hospital
A&E
25
Heath Rd
Rushmere Heath
Golf Club

The Drift
Melton Road
Caudle Rd
Ringham
Upland Rd
Springland Cl
Mandy Close
Crabbe Street
Cowper Street
Sunfield Close
Bloomfield St
Britannia Road
Halliwell Road
Thanet Rd
Brisbane Rd
Ditchingham
Blackdown

A B C D E

48

6 21 22

The Courts

Church Lane

Church

The Mdw

Hill Farm Road

Brook Lane

Hill House

Fynn Valley Walk

Playford

Richards Drive

Michaels Mount

Holly Close

Lane

Sandy Lane

Bealing School

Little Bealings

I

Fynn Valley Walk

Fynn

2

New Buildings

Mallard Business

Beacon Hil

47

Playford Road

Lux Farm

3

19

Lane

Pla

Rushmere Street

Playford Road

4

Doctor Watson's Lane

re Street

46

IP5

Playford Heath

Kesgrave High School

5

Bent Lane

Mead Meadowside

Gardens

The Maples

Woodbridge Road

A1214

MAIN ROAD

Main Road

Alberta Close

Edmonton Drive

Quebec Drive

St Lawrence Way

Mackenzie Drive

Cambridge Road

Grantchester Place

Cariton Road

The Walk

Bell Lane

Chrch Cl

Heath Primary School

Ferguson

St Olaves Road

St Olaves Drive

MAIN ROAD

PO

Windrush Road

Emerald Close

Ashdale Road

Wainwright Way

Wright Lane

Turner

Ropes

Cranwell Grove

Gardens

Harpo Grove

Scopes Grove

Ruby Cl

Cardew

Fentons Way

Fentons Way

Dewar Lane

Fairbairn Avenue

Knights Lane

Elmers Lane

Dri

Beech Gv

Elm Road

Holly Road

Trinity Close

Chester Road

Oxford Road

Edmonton Close

Laurel Avenue

Michigan Close

Camborne

Ropes Drive

Cranwell Grove

Shr Fld

Dodson Vale

Deben Road

Willetrie Drive

Sheppards Way

Knights Lane

Ropes

The Tyds

Curls Way

Century Dr

6

Linksfield Gardens

Linksfield

Beech Road

Quan Close

St Agnes Wy

Orchard Grove

Montana Road

Columbia Close

Felix Close

Penryn Road

Surgery

Mead Dr

Twelve Acre Approach

Rowarth

Dodson Vale

Lummis Vale

Spinder Cl

Century Dr

Kesgrave

ROAD

2 45

Men Drive

Backdown Aven

St Agnes Wy

St Austell Close

Cedar Avenue

Penza

Oregon Road

St Ives Close

Falmouth Close

Baird Gv

Cox Cl

Cock Gdns

Halls Drift

Wilkinson Drive

Walk Cha

Pegay Lane

Bull

Col Ter

Castle

Cedarwood Primary School

Filbrigg Av

Barnham Place

Bodmin Close

Padstow

Heath

S M Cl

The Garrods

Kingsl

A B **26** C D E

1 grid square represents 500 metres

Golf Centre
Seckford
Golf Course

F　G　H　14　J　K

24　25　B14

48

The Grove

Fynn Valley Walk
Fynn Valley Walk

A12

Brock La
Top St

I

River Fynn

Fynn Va Wk
Top St

Sand

LC

Beacon Lane
Martlesham Road
Martlesham Road

Bealings
Road

The Street

2

School Lane

47

Hall Road

Martlesham

Rechwood Close
Valley Vw Ri
Nunn Cl
Private Rd

Viking Cl
Viking Heights

C

3

Green La
Alban Cl
Alban Sq
Sq

Bkcom Cl
Chandos Chat
Chase
'dos' Court
Drive

Ravens Ww

Holfen
Close

W

Martlesham
Beacon Hill
Primary School

Blackfurs Lane

Angela Cl

Private
Road

Shaw la Rd

Main Road

The Ryes School
Organisation

Kesgrave
Hall

PO
Carol
Avenue
Angela Close

Crown
Cl

Main Road

Nunn

4

P+

Main Road

Felixstowe

46

MAIN ROAD

Portal Avenue

Superstore

5

214

Bracken Avenue

Dobbs Lane

Deben Avenue

Peel
Yard

The Paddocks

The

Anson

Beardmore Park

Woodside

Anson Vw
Ason Vw
The Av
The Drive
Genova Av
Lusano Av

Wards Vw

Squires
Lane

Demesne
Gardens

Way

Mahon
Road

Martinsyde

Rema Av
Turino Av

Howards
Way

Jolly

Sargent Grove

Stephen Road

Gayfer Avenue

Brkers Place
The Grove

Cafford Close

Manor Road

The Chase

Hnts
Cl

Hilton Road

Hawker Dr

Gloster Road

Fox Lea
Francis Cr
Magnall Walk
Mo Page

Grange Close
Grange Lane

Dobbs Lane

Copswood Close

Whinfield

Eagle Close

Saddlers Place

Hers Close

Betts Avenue

Works

Herbert Road

Stmmrs Pl
The Bretts

Buzby Way

Gorseland Primary School

Drift

Broomfield

Broomfield Mews

Valliant Road

The Drift

PO
Surgery

count

Bgss
Pl

6

Hartree Way

Haskins Walk
Tommy Flowers
Turing Ct

Terry Ct
Goodman
Terry
Tremlett
Vincent
Gans

Eagle Way

Warren Lane

Birchwood County Primary Sch

Swan Close

Barrack Square

245

Jeavons Lane

Peacock
W V Cl
Galley Av Cl
Terry Gardens

Howlett's

Terry Gardens

Harvest Way

Undnside

Forest Lane

Coopers Road

Eagle Way

Rise

Avocet Cl

25

F　G　H　27　J　K

Pine Bank

The Oaks

Holly End

ch grove

Martlesham Heath

A1214

Eagle Way

A   **B**   16   **C**   **D**   **E**

6 | | | 2

Farm

The Grind

Gipping

Lower St

Sproughton Rd

Sproughton

Perry Barn

Laurel Farm

Burstall Lane

Beech Close

Church Crs

Church St

Samford Place

Glebe Cl

Broomfield Common

Gipping Wy

I

Abbey Oaks

Oak CV

Ransome Close

Monks Gate

HIGH STREET

Church Lane

Sproughton CE Primary School

Burstall Lane

Abbey Oaks Farm

2

45

44

HURDLE MAKERS HILL

Ivywell Farm

A1071

A1071

B1113

Springvale

3

A1071

Fen Farm

Burstall Bridge

A14

4

Valley Farm

Belstead Brook

Swan Hill

Poplar Farm

Poplar Lane

Pigeon's Lane

43

Pigeon's Lane

The Grange

Washbrook Street

Pigeon's Lane

A1214

LON

5

Spring Road

P+

Swan Hill

London Road

Scrivener

Cherry Rd

Superstore

Amor Hall

The Marvens

London Road

A14

Superstore

Oldfield Rd

Cottingham Rd

6

Washbrook

Fen Farm

Chapel Lane

Whights' Corner

Cottingham Rd

42

Charlotte

Street

Mill La

Pearsons Wy

PO

Pineasant Rd

paddock

nary School

London Road

School Hill

Mill Lane

J55

A   **B**   30   **C**   **D**   **E**

Fen Vw Back

Dales Vw

Fen Vw

6 | | | 2

Road

Farthing Road Industrial Estate

Sproughton Road

Business Park

Gipping Valley River Path

Riverside

NORWICH ROAD

Boss Hall Rd

Superstore

Boss Hall

Baird Road

Hadleigh Road Ind Est

Whitton Road

Handford Hall Primary Sch

Suffolk Retail Park

Works

Elton Park Industrial Est

Brookhouse Business Park

New Superstore

Sikh Temple

YARMOUTH RD

Business Cen

Hadleigh Road

Allenby Rd

LONDON RD

A137

Cullingham Rd

HANDFORD ROAD

Portmans Wk Industrial Cen

Elton Park

Nine Acres

Hyntle

Anita Cl East

Pickwick Rd

Dickens Road

Copperfield Close

Dombey

St Paul's

Orwell Retail Park

Ranelagh Primary Sch

Bus Depot

WEST END RD

Barker Close

Ventris Cl

Orchard Gate

Collinson's

West

Anita Cl

Lavenham Rd

Kelly Road

A1214

Lavenham Rd

Columbine Gdns

Iris Cl

RANELAGH ROAD B1075

Retail Park

Works

Red House

Hadleigh Road

Chantry Park

Milden Road

Lupin Road

Coltsfoot Rd

Consild

Poppy Close

Waller's

Grove

Gippeswyk Park

Gippeswyk Avenue

LONDON ROAD

Curlew Road

Buddleia Close

Orchid Close

Crocus Close

Lavender Hill

Yarebell

Primrose Close

Clover Close

Violet Close

Campion Rd

Birkfield Close

Tram

Aster

Bluebell Close

Cornflower

Thistle Close

Speedwell

Ancaste Rd

Queenscliffe Road

Oaks Community Primary School

Shamrock Av

Marigold

Daffodil Close

Pimpernel

Hawthorn Dr

Sorrel

Maple

St Marks RC Primary Sch

Birkfield Drive

Stone Lodge

Belstead Road

Wren Av

Teal Cl

Partridge Road

Kingfisher Av

Chantry

Surg

Pelican Close

Way

Hawthorn Way

Stone Lodge Lane West

Beacon Hill Special School

IP2

Heatherhayes

Fernhayes

Chantry Clnc

Chantry High School

St Josephs College

Swallow

Robin Drive

Greenfinch Road

Kestrel Road

Woodpecker Drive

Gannet Road

Sheldrake Drive

Kittiwake Drive

Pintail Close

Tern Road

Mallard

Birkfield Drive

Merlin Cl

Goldcrest Road

Hawthorn

Sprites La

Denton

Royston Dr

Whitworth Close

Middleton Close

Fitzwilliam Cl

Emmanuel Close

Belstead Road

Sprites Primary School

Didsbury

Worsley Close

Manchester Rd

Lakeside

Dunlin

Plover Road

Birkfield Drive

Magdalene Close

The Willows Primary School

Sandringham Cl

Prince

Minrow

Ashton

Bridgwater Road

Sandpiper Drive

Newnham Ct

Peterhouse Close

Wales

Wilmslow Drive

Holcombe Crs

Monton Rd

Atherton Road

Cambridge Drive

Girton Way

Balmoral Close

Stoke Park Drive

Surgery

Glamorgan

Eccles Road

Iram Rd

Annbrook Road

Birkfield

St Catherines Rd

Belstead Road

Wigmore Close

Neath Drive

Yewtree

Belmont

Pin Mill Cl

Pendleton

Bramhall

Ellenbrook Road

Ritabrook Rd

Carolbrook Road

Gusford Primary School

Badgers Bank

Eglestone Road

Leicester Close

Stoke Park

Fountains

Bowland Dr

Baldry Close

Wardley Close

Swinton Close

Appleby Close

Brookview

Furness Road

Bourne Park

Corporation

Dashwood Close

Ellenbrook Rd

Marbled

Downside Cl

Winchester Wy

Park Drive

Belstead

1 grid square represents 500 metres

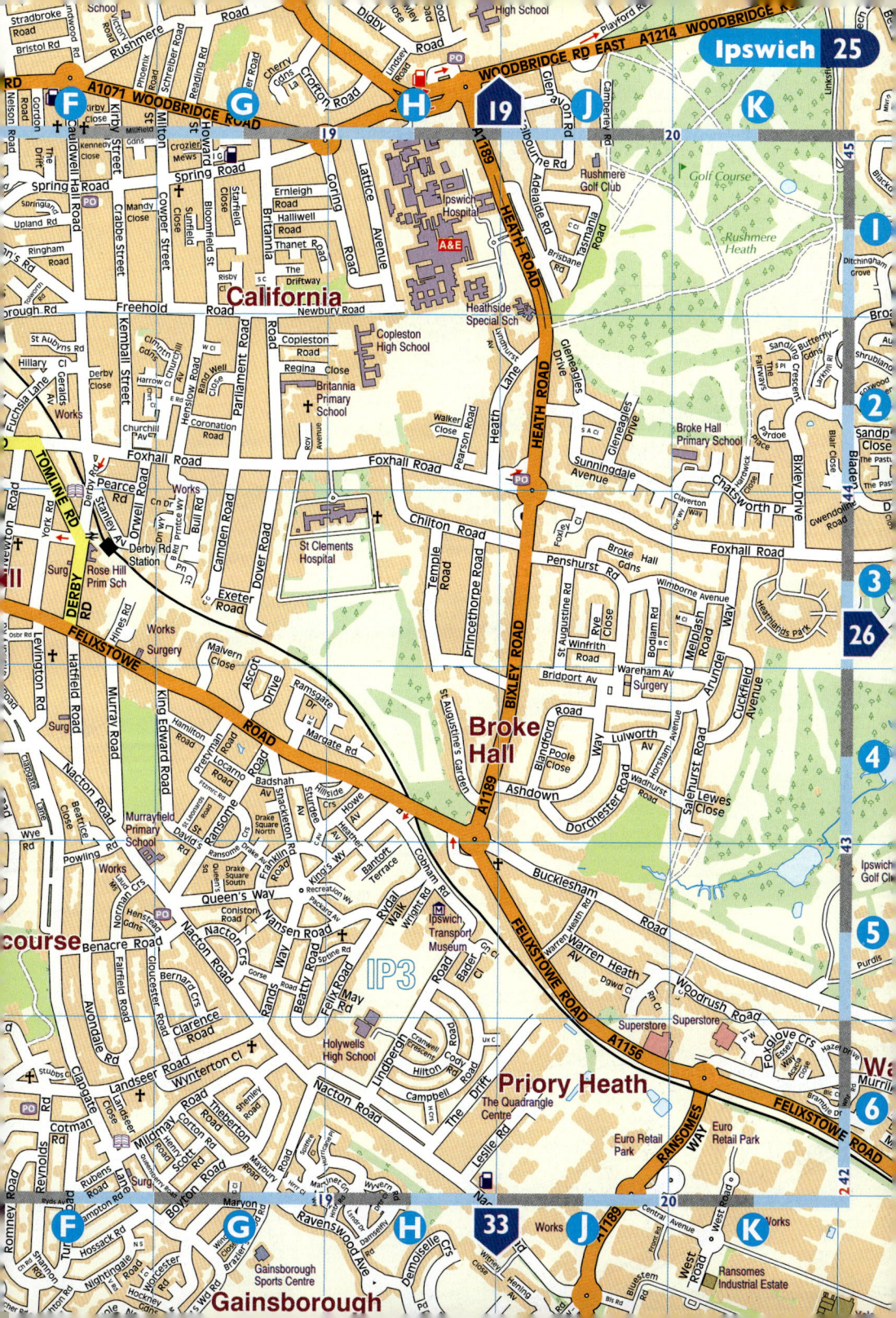

A1071 WOODBRIDGE ROAD

WOODBRIDGE RD EAST A1214 WOODBRIDGE

California

Ipswich Hospital

A&E

Heathside Special Sch

Copleston High School

Britannia Primary School

Rushmere Golf Club

Golf Course

Rushmere Heath

Broke Hall Primary School

St Clements Hospital

Derby Rd Station

Rose Hill Prim Sch

Broke Hall

Penshurst Rd

Foxhall Road

Heathlands Park

Murrayfield Primary School

Drake Square North

Drake Square South

Queen's Way

Recreation

IP3

Ipswich Transport Museum

Holywells High School

Priory Heath

The Quadrangle Centre

Euro Retail Park

Euro Retail Park

Superstore

Superstore

Ipswich Golf Club

Purdis

Gainsborough Sports Centre

Gainsborough

Ransomes Industrial Estate

FELIXSTOWE ROAD A1156

RANSOMES WAY

West Road

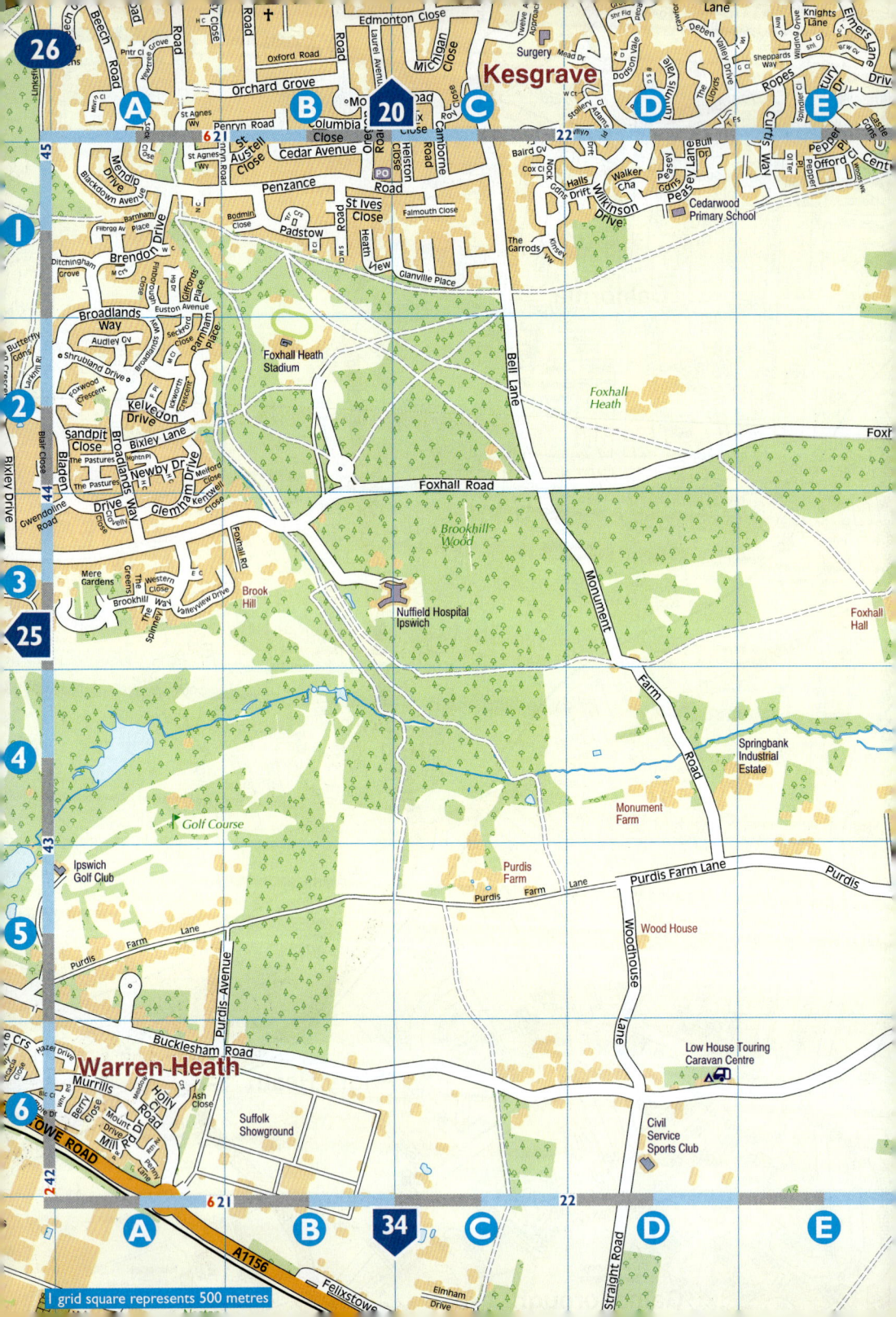

26 45

A B 20 C D E

Kesgrave

Surgery
Cedarwood Primary School

Oxford Road
Orchard Grove
Edmonton Close
Laurel Avenue

St Agnes Wy
Penryn Road
Columbia Close
Cedar Avenue
St Austell Close
Camborne
Michigan Close
Heston Close

I

Mendip Drive
Blackdown Avenue
Brendon Drive
Penzance Road
Bodmin Close
Padstow
St Ives Close
Falmouth Close
The Garrods
Glanville Place
Wilkinson Drive
Walker Cha
Pepsey Lane

Broadlands Way
Audley Cv
Shrubland Drive
Foxwood Crescent
Euston Avenue
Farnham Place
Foxhall Heath Stadium
Foxhall Heath
Bell Lane

2 44

Sandpit Close
The Pastures
Bixley Lane
Newby Dr
Kelvedon Drive
Broadlands Way
Glemham Way
Foxhall Rd
Bixley Drive
Gwendoline Road
Foxhall Road
Brookhill Wood

3

Mere Gardens
The Greens
Western Close
Valleyview Drive
Brook Hill
Brookhill
The Spinney
Nuffield Hospital Ipswich
Monument Farm Road
Foxhall Hall

25

4 43

Golf Course
Springbank Industrial Estate

Ipswich Golf Club
Monument Farm
Purdis Farm
Purdis Farm Lane
Purdis

5

Purdis Farm Lane
Purdis Avenue
Wood House
Woodhouse Lane

Bucklesham Road
Low House Touring Caravan Centre

Warren Heath
Murrills
Holly Road
Ash Close
Suffolk Showground
Civil Service Sports Club

6

FELIXSTOWE ROAD
A1156 Felixstowe
Straight Road
Elmham Drive

A 34 B C D E

1 grid square represents 500 metres

F G H 21 J K

Hartree Way
Seavons Lane
Walk
Peacock
Terry Gardens
Tremlett
Vincent
Goodman

Westland
Eagle Way
Vaillant Rd
The Drift
Surgery
PO
Birchwood County Primary Sch
Coopers Road
Eagle Way
Barrack Square
Avocet Lane
Avocet Lane

I 45

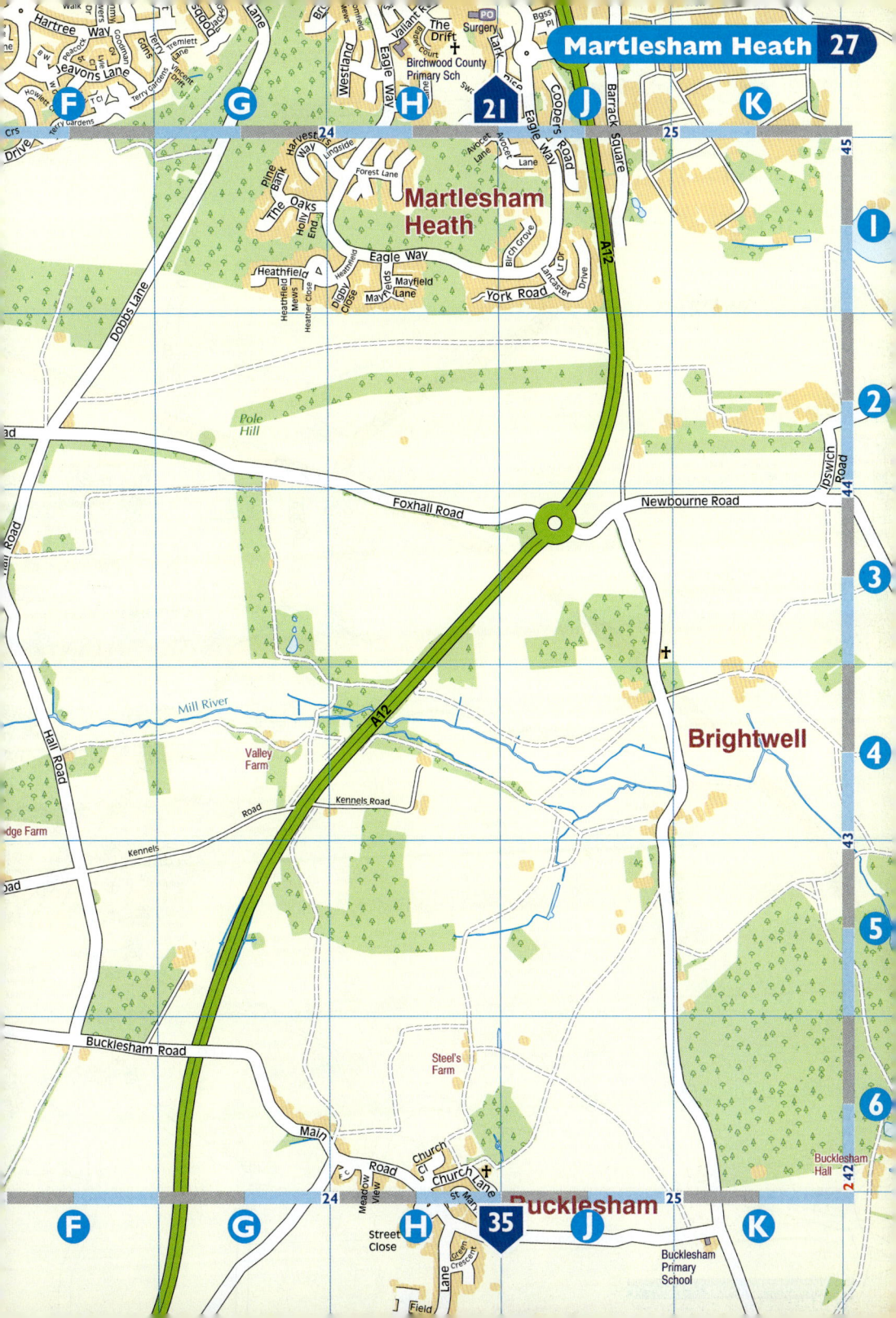

Martlesham Heath

Pine Bank Way
The Oaks
Harvest Way
Lingside
Forest Lane
Holly End

Heathfield Mews
Heathfield
Digby Close
Mayne
Heather Close
Mayfield Lane
Spire

Eagle Way
York Road
Birch Grove
Lancaster Drive

Dobbs Lane

Pole Hill

Foxhall Road
Newbourne Road

2 44 Ipswich Road

3

Mill River
Hall Road
Valley Farm

Brightwell

4 43

Kennels Road
Road

odge Farm
Kennels
oad

5

Bucklesham Road

6 2 42 Bucklesham Hall

Steel's Farm

Main Road
Meadow View
Church Ct
Church Lane
St. Mary

Street Close
Lane
Crescent
Field

Bucklesham

Bucklesham Primary School

F G H 35 J K

24 25 24 25

A **601** B Mill Hill C Cytree D E

Ivytree Farm
Cosford Hall
Cosford

I
Mill Lane
44
Mill Lane
Noaks Tye Farm
A1141
River Brett
Peyton Hall

2
Water Lane
Lane
STONE STREET
A1071
Aldham Mill Hill
IP7

3
43
A1071
B1070
GALLOWS HL
Gallows Hl
Castle Rd
Castle Rd
Castle Rd
Castle
Woodlands
Ann Beaumont Wy
Ann Beaumont Wy
Ann
Sun Court
Chsnll
Oxford Rd
Emm'sn Wy
Durrant Rd
Beau Scho
Boswell Lan
Rampling Cl
Freeman Cl
Bradfield
Bradfie
Church

4
Coram Street
Friars Hall Farm
Friars Rd
Corks Lane
Council Building
BRIDGE ST
Brett Works
HIGH STREET
Calais Street
Pykenham Wy
Pykenham Wy
Meadow Wy
Spooners Cl
Inkerman Cl
Cncl Bldg
ANGEL STREET
Maadalen Rd
Guthum Rd

Constitutional Hill
Pound La
Church St
Fozel Thtr
The Guildhall
Health Cen
Corn Exchange
Market Pl
Silk Mill Cl
Duke St

5
STREET
A1071 STREET
Park Farm
Holbecks
Lane
Toppesfield Cl
Hadleig Primar School
B1u

242

6
Holbecks
Laviham Rd
Tinker's La
Raven Wy
Hadleigh RUFC

A **601** B C **02** D E W
Pott's Farm
Hill Farm

I grid square represents 500 metres

F G Church Lane The H J K

04 05

Aldham Hall

I

Wolves Wood Nature Reserve

44

Lane

Wolves Farm

2

A1071 IPSWICH ROAD Wolves Farm The Montessori School IPSWICH ROAD A1071

Cobbolds Farm

Red Hill Road Red Hill Road Crockatt Road Malvon

Lady Lane Industrial Estate

Lady Lane

B1070 Ramsey Rd Delf Cl

3

43

Hadleigh

B1070 New Cut The Gn Tower Mill La

Valley Farm

4

St Marys Primary School Edwin Parks Road Frog Hall Lane Frog Hall

French's Farm

Lane

Woolner Close Hadleigh High School

Highlands Road Road Woodthorpe Road Glanville Road Cranworth Rd

5

42

Pond Hall Road Works Valley Pond Hall Farm Pond Hall

Pond Hall Road Hadleigh Business Park Works Pond Hall Rd Clay

6

Hook Lane

Town House Fruit Farm

F STREET G 04 H J 05 K

Hadleigh Railway Walk Kate's Hill Farm

Washbrook

A Fen Farm   **B**   22   **C**   **D** Whights' Corner   **E**

Superstore

A1214

Cole's Rd

Chapel Lane

Mill La

The Street

Pearsons Wy

PO

Mill Lane

J55

42

611

12

Church Lane

Hollow Road

Copdock Primary School

School Hill

London Road

Pound

I

Fen Vw Back Lane

Dales Vw

Fen Vw

Elm Lane

Saxon Lane

Wenham Road

Copdock

Copdock CC

Lane

Belstead Hall

2

41

Mace Green

The Hotel Elizabeth

The Avenue

Oakfield Road

Church La

Buck's

Horns

3

A12

4

Redhouse Farm

40

Folly Lane

Lane Farm

Brockley Wood

Old Hall Wood

5

A12

Travelodge

J32b

Bentley Old Hall

6

London Road

Bentley Long Wood

Old Hall Lane

Bentley Manor

239

611

12

A   **B** 39   **C**   **D**   **E**

Pond Hall

1 grid square represents 500 metres

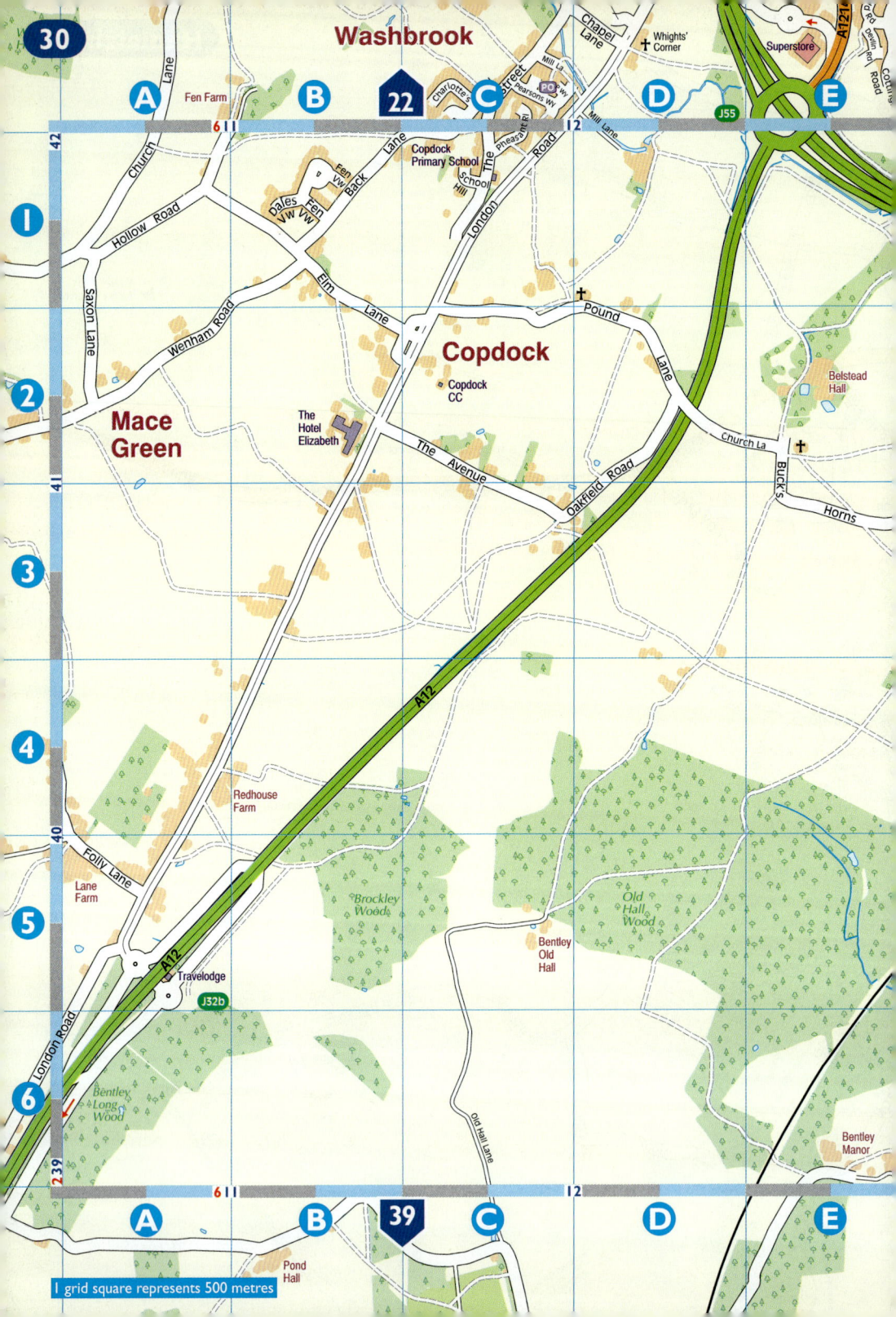

F | G | H | 23 | J | K

Yew Tree
Belmont
Pin
Brammat
Gusford Primary School
Appleby Close
Sycamore
Rudlands
Wardley Close
Linton Close
Ellenbrook Road
Quilter
Baldry Dr
shortacres
St Catherine
Carolbrook Road
Rd
Ribabt
Trilabrook
Grebbook
Bainbridge
Clifton Way
Belstead Road
Stoke Park
Dashwood Close
Grove Hill
Swilowt Cl
Skipper
Trellt
Brimstone Rd
Brookview
Stoke Park Drive
Furness Cl
Newgt
Jester
Downside
Fountains
Stoke Pk
Corporation
Bourne Park
Ellenbrook Rd
Marbled White
Burnet Close
Clearwing
Cabr
Springgt
Cooper
Forester
Holly Blue Cl
Mayfly
Lwngt
CV
Belstead Brook
Alderlee
Winchester W
Whitland Close
Abbotsbury Ct
I

Holly Lane
Grove Hill
A14
Bobbits Lane
Bobbits Lane
2

Chapel Lane
Grove Hill
Belstead
Thorington Hall
41
3

Grove
Blacksmith's Corner
The Street
32

The B Ce

Pannington Hall
A137
4

Vicara

Bluegate Farm
40
5

A137
Valley
Lane
6

Hubbard's Hall Farm
Park House
2 39

F | G | 14 | H | J | 15 | K

Holbrook Park

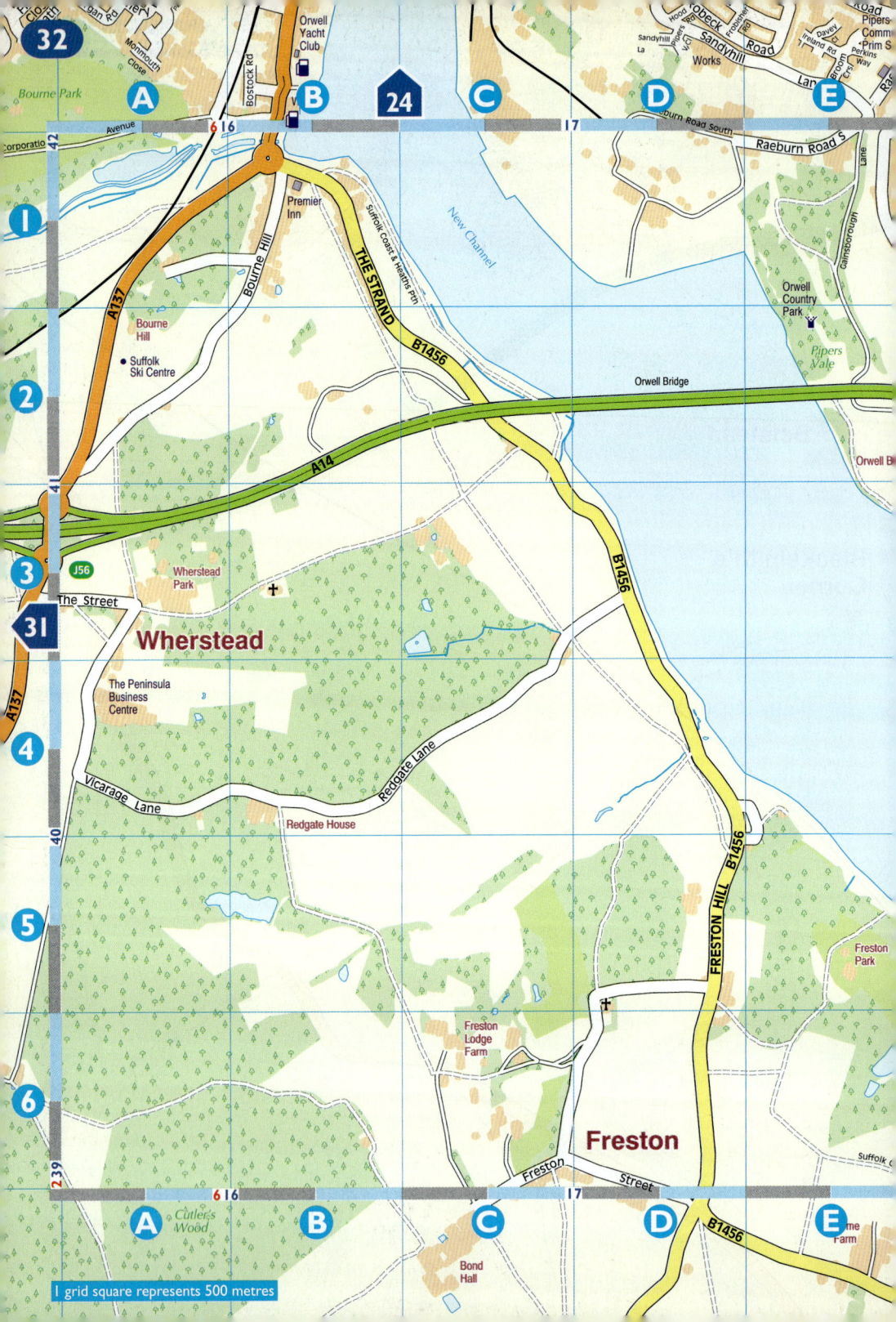

A **B** 24 **C** **D** **E**

Monmouth Close
oan Rd
Clo
Hill
Corporatio
Avenue
6 16
42
41

Orwell Yacht Club
Bostock rd

Bourne Park

Sandyhill
Sandyhill
Obeck
Road
Pipers
Comm
Prim
Works
Pipers
Road
Lane
Davey
Ireland Rd
Perkins
Way

Bourn Road South
Raeburn Road S
Lane
Gainsborough

1 7

Premier Inn

THE STRAND

Bourne Hill

New Channel

Suffolk Coast & Heaths Ptn

Orwell Country Park

Pipers Vale

Bourne Hill

B1456

Orwell Bridge

Orwell B

2

Suffolk Ski Centre

A14

3 J56

The Street

B1456

31

Wherstead Park

Wherstead

Orwell B

A137

The Peninsula Business Centre

4

Vicarage Lane

Redgate House

Redgate Lane

B1456

Freston Hill

40

5

Freston Park

Freston

6

Freston Lodge Farm

Freston Hill B1456

2 39

6 16

Cutler's Wood

1 7

Freston Street

Freston

A **B** **C** **D** B1456 **E**
me Farm

Bond Hall

1 grid square represents 500 metres

Priory Heath

The Quadrangle Centre

Euro Retail Park
Euro Retail Park

25

F **G** **H** **J** **K**

Nacton Road

Works
Works

Central Avenue

West Road

Ransomes Industrial Estate

Demoiselle Crs
Hening

Bluestem Road

Gainsborough

Gainsborough Sports Centre

Ravenswood Ave

Bonny Crs

Ravenswood Av

NACTON ROAD

Foxtail Rd

Bluestem Road

I

Yale Busine Park

Ravenswood Community Prim School

Downham Rd
Downham Blvd

Manstrook

Hanne Rd

Bermuda Road

Foxtail Road

The Havens

Courtyard by Marriott Hotel

Alnesbourn Crs

Alnesbourn

Cranberry square

Suffolk Coast & Heaths Path

A1

2

Ipswich Airport (disused)

J57

Morland Primary School

Pond Hall Farm

A14

Ips

3

34

Priory Park

Bridge Wood

Alnesbourne Priory Golf Club

Goldsmith's Covert

4

Golf Course

Park Farm

5

River Orwell

6

Mannings Lane
Pratts Lane

Suffolk Coast & Heaths Path

40

Hall Point

Ipswich High School

F **G** **H** **J** **K**

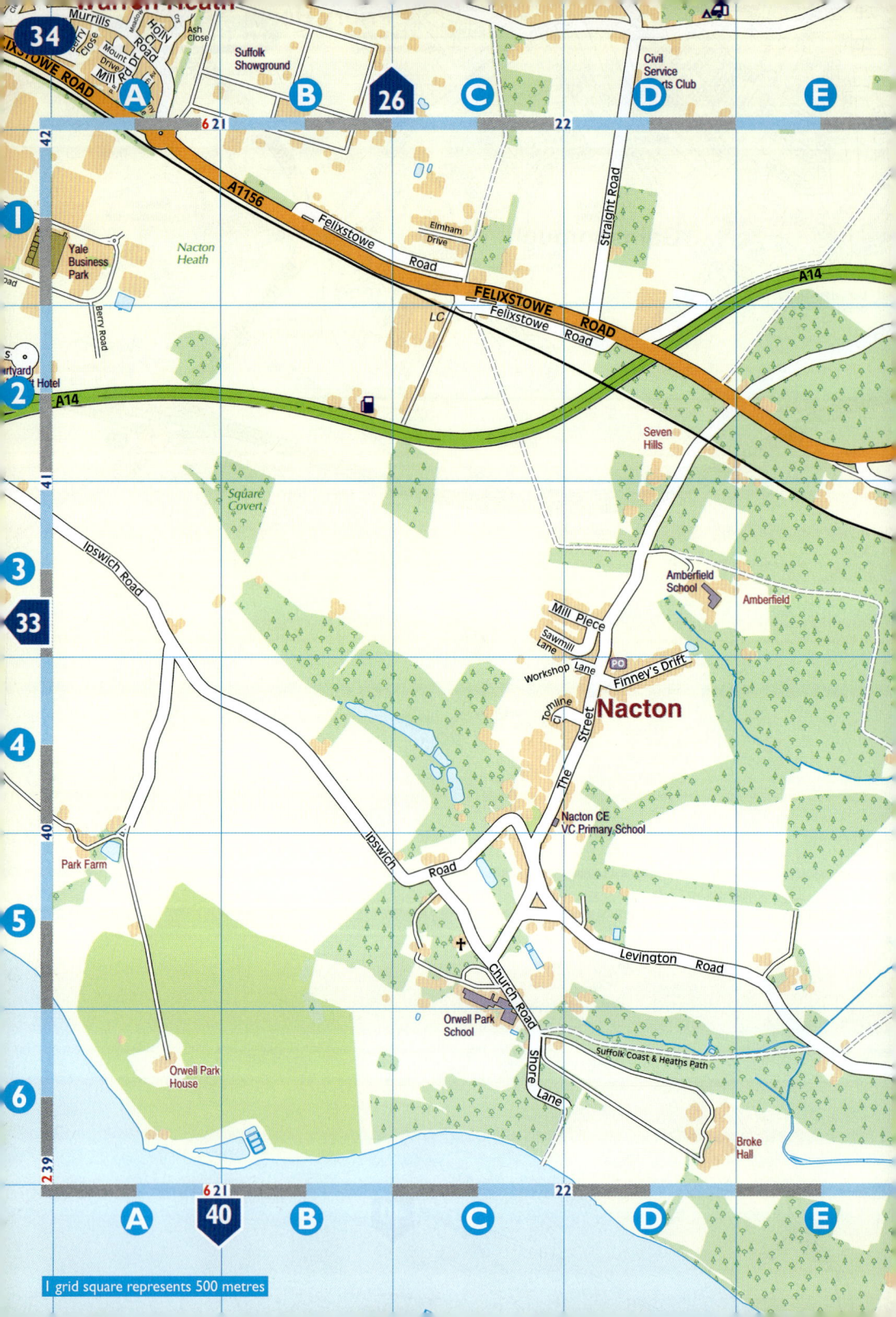

Grid references: 34, 26, 42, 41, 40, 33, 39, 22, 6 21, 2

Roads and features:
- TASTOWE ROAD / FELIXSTOWE ROAD
- A1156
- A14
- Felixstowe Road
- Elmham Drive
- Straight Road
- Berry Road
- Ipswich Road
- Mill Piece
- Sawmill Lane
- Workshop Lane
- Tomline
- Finney's Drift
- The Street
- Levington Road
- Church Road
- Shore Lane

Places:
- Warren Heath
- Murrills
- Holly Road
- Mount Drive
- Ash Close
- Suffolk Showground
- Civil Service Sports Club
- Yale Business Park
- Nacton Heath
- Hotel
- Seven Hills
- Square Covert
- Amberfield School
- Amberfield
- Nacton
- PO
- Nacton CE VC Primary School
- Park Farm
- Orwell Park School
- Orwell Park House
- Suffolk Coast & Heaths Path
- Broke Hall
- LC
- S
- rtyard

A–E column markers (top and bottom), **I, 2, 3, 4, 5, 6 row markers**

1 grid square represents 500 metres

F G H J K

Bucklesham

Main Road
Meadow View
Church Lane
St Mary's Pk
Green Crescent
Street Farm Close
Field View
Lane
Slip Ponds
Levington

27

25

Bucklesham Hall

I

Bucklesham Primary School

2

Heath Cottages

IP10

41

Ten

Tenth Road

Redhouse Farm

3

Levington Lane

Levington Heath

A14

4

40

5

36

Walk Farm

A14

Red House Walk

Bridge Road

LC

6

239

Levington

Felixstowe Road

Bridge Road

Church Lane
PH

24

Strattonhall D

25

F **41** G H J K

lk Coast & eaths Path

Stratton Hall

A 6 26 B C 27 D E

I

40

2

35

3

39

4

5

2 38

6

A 6 26 B C 27 D E

Road

Bucklesham

Road

Bucklesham Road

Bucklesham Road

Strustton Rd

Weir
We
Pla

Burnt Hou

Kirt

Rectory

Meadow

Oakdene

Croft
Farm

Trimley Road

Innocence Lane

Innocence Lane

Croft House

Kirton Road

Trimley St Martin
Primary School

Morston Hall Road

LC

Morston
Hall

A14

**Trimley
St Martin**

Heathfields

Mill Close

Red House Cl

Capel
Close

Sandy
Close

CAVENDISH
Lane

Mill

Suffolk Coast & Heaths Pth

LC

Kirton Road

A14

Old Kirton Road

Blue Barn

Craig

Jasmine

St Martins Green

**Thorpe
Common**

Thorpe Lane

Grimston

High Rd

Brick Kiln
Close

1 grid square represents 500 metres

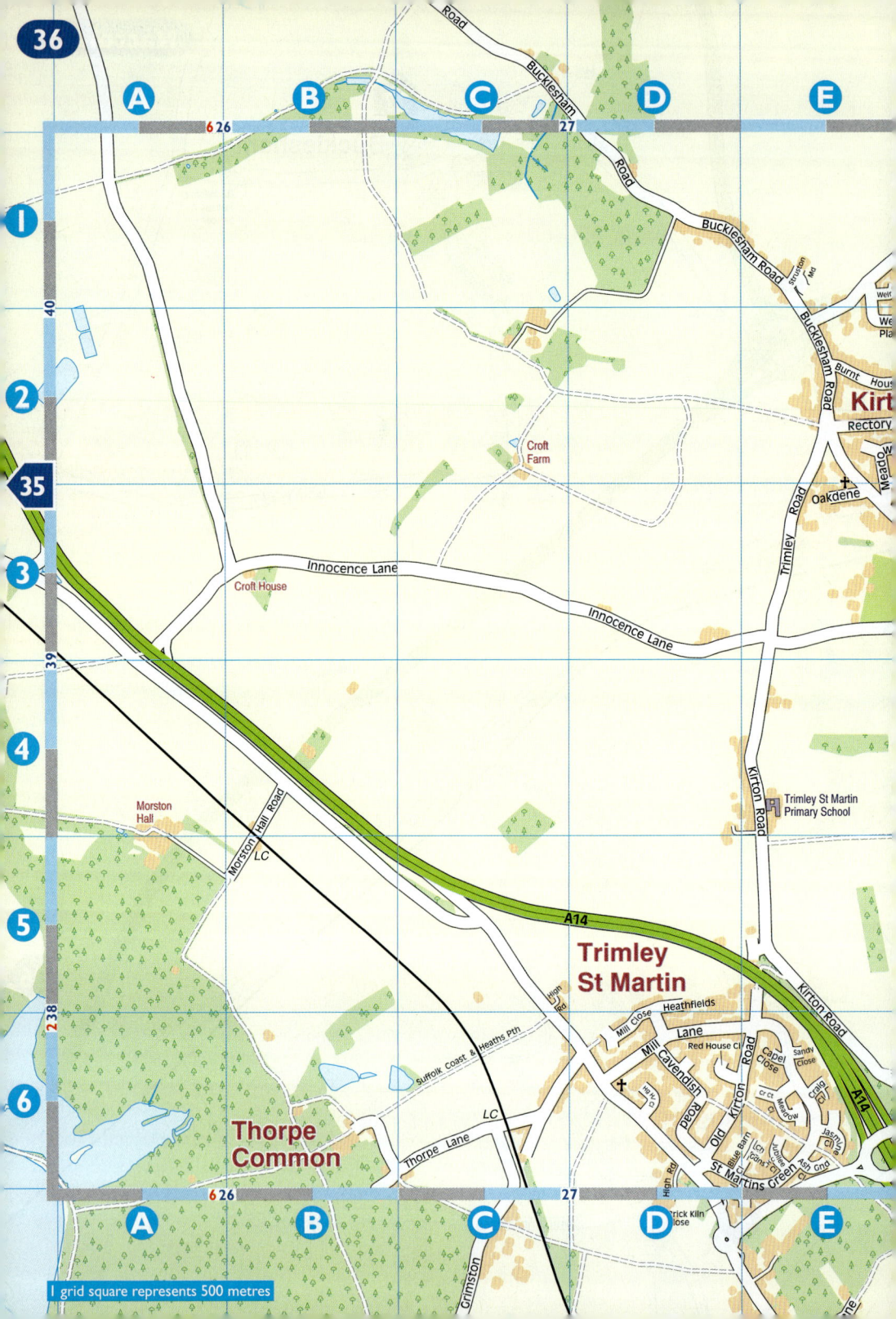

F G H J K

29 30

I

40

2

Falkenham Sink

Croxton

Gdns

Gray's Orch

Road

Falkenham Road

Falkenham

Lower Falkenham Rd

Red House Farm

3

39

Sheepgate Lane

4

Lower Falkenham

Back Lane

Lower Road

Suffolk Coast & Heaths Path

5

Lane

Brook

Suffolk Coast & Heaths Path

Deben Lodge Farm

Back Lane

Back Lane

2 38

Capel Hall Lane

6

Capel Hall Lane

29 30

Capel Hall

Church

The Drift

Lane

Church La

A　B　C　D　E

39

07　08　09

I

Grove Farm

Little Wenham

Jermyns Farm

Gipsy Row

Brook　　Lane

Days Road

Capel St Mary

Churchford Hall

Windmill Hill

Mill Hill

Mill Cl

Days Green

Dawes Close

Catesbray

Thorney

Ash Gv

Crotchets Close

Penny Meadow

Peter's Grove

Ryland Rd

Shop Precinct

Boydlands

snowcroft

Capel St Mary School

The Street

Cedars Lane

Plough Road

Chapel

Link Rd

Letton Close

Stockners End

Bustle Close

smithers

Rembrow

Smewers

Chalkners Cl.

Little Close

2

38

Wenham Place

Pound Lane

Capelgrove

Red Lane

3

Wenham Lane

Wenham Hill

37

4

Road

Bluegate

Pound Lane

Old　London

Manor House

5

A12

Lattinford Hill

Chaplain's Farm

31

6

Cutlers Lane

Woodgates Road

Woodgates Farm

Cutlers Lane

2 36

07　08　09

A　B　45　C　D　E

Barn Business Centre

East

Hall

Bentley
Long
Wood

London

F G H **30** J K

10 11 12 39

Pond
Hall

Bentley
Park

I

Glebe Road
R Rd
JF Cl
The Pightie
Penn Close
Little
Tufts
Great Tufts

London Rd

The Street

Travelodge

J32a

Butcher's Lane

White
Horse
La
Mowlands Rd
Homefield
Long
Perry
Rd
Road

Friars
London

A12

Church Road

†

2

38

3

Potash Lane

Grove
Farm

Falslaff
Manor

Potash

Church Road

4

37

Bentley Primary
School

Tawneys
Farm

Case Lane

Bentley

West Mill
Garden
South Vw Gn
East Mill
Gn
Highfields

The
Link

Link Lane

Station Road

Grove Rd

Church Road

silver ley

LC

5

236

6

Dodnash
Wood

Martins
Glen

10 11 12

F G **46** H J K

Dodn
Priory
Farm

Coppey
Farm

A   B   **33**   C   D   E

20

619

21

39

I

Cat House

Hall Point

Suffolk Coast & Heaths Path

Ipswich High School

Woolverstone Park

Suffolk Coast & Heaths Path

2

38

Pin Mill

Suffolk Coast & Heaths Path

B1456

3

MAIN ROAD

Richardsons Lane

Orwell Rise

Pinmill Road

Chelmondiston

Woodlands

Chelmondiston CP School

Collimer Cl

Rectory Field

Wendy Close

Hollow La

Hill Farm La

Walnut Tree Farm

Mil La

St Andrew's Dr

Church St

4

37

Bylam Lane

B1456   MAIN   ROAD

PO

Ling's Lane

5

49

Bylam Farm

6

Grove

236

619

Ling's Lane

Grove Lane

Lane

20   21

A   B   C   D   E

Lovers Lane

The Vale

1 grid square represents 500 metres

F **34** **G** **H** **J** **K**

Levington **35**

hore Lane

Coast & Heaths Path

Broke Hall

Church Lane

Strattonhall

Suffolk Coast & Heaths Path

I

River

2

Orwell

3

Clamp House

4

Wade's Lane

5

B1456

Red House Farm

Hill House

Charity Farm

Pear Tree Farm

Church End

6

Boot Drift

Shotley Hall

Frogs Alley

Church Walk

Frogs Alley

F **G** **50** **H** **J** **K**

B1456

42

A14

J59

36

6 28

29

St Martins Green

Old

Blue Barn

Ash

Capel Hall Lane

Capel Hall

Capel Lane

I

37

Church Lane

High Road

PO

Thurmans Lane

Candlet

Hill House Farm

Gulpher Business Park

2

Garners Lane

Laud's Cl

Stennett's Cl

Surgery

Drovers

Brotherton Av

Dawson Dr

Faulkeners

The Josselyns

Thomas Rd

Meadow

Fen

Way

Manor Road

St Mary's Rd

Mt Pouch

A14

Langston's

Puncnard Way

Hunters End

Crer

Wheelwrights

LC

3

Trimley St Mary

Keelers Lane

36

The Avenue

Second Av

Station New Road

Trimley St Mary Primary School

Black Barns

Burnham Cl

Dains Pl

Addington Road

Eaton

El Gdns

Farriers Went

Myers Gn

Spriteshall

High Road

Eastland Cl

Spriteshall Lane

J60

CANDLET ROAD

A154

Treetops

Ascot Drive

Gulpher Road

Cowpa Farm

Road

4

P

Searson's Farm

Trimley Station

Chatsworth Crs

IP11

Hawes Lane

High Street

Falcon Street

Church Lane

St Mary's Lane

Ataka Rd

Surgery Road

Longcroft

Causton Junior School

Maidstone Road

King Street

Crown St

Alexandra Road

Queen

PO

The Walk

Recreation La

Exm Road

Walton

Clickett Hill

PORT OF FELIXSTOWE ROAD

Rumacles

Way

Winston Cl

Avenue

Orwell High Sch

Maidstone Rd

Margaret St

Cape Rd

Graham Rd

Seaton Road

Chepstow Rd

Kentsley Rd

Chester Rd

Exeter Rd

West

Devon

5

2 35

Hintlesham

Mellis Cl

Farm

Hall Fld

Garden Fld

Hall Pond

Recreation Gound

Maidstone Infant School

Cornwall Road

Lawn

Shrubbery

Nursery Walk

Deben High School

Walk

Valley

6

Blofield Road

Nicholas Rd

Anzani Av

J61

Blofield Rd

A14

A154

AVENUE A154

Grange

Superstore

Surg

Grange Primary School

Cricket Hi

Parkeston Road

Langley Cemetery

Selvale Way

Thorn Way

Playing Field

Langley Cl

Felixstowe Cemetery

Coyfield Avenue

Newry Av

Surrey Lane

Carrison Lane

Mill

Fagbury

Parker

Avenue

Ferry

Dooley

52

6 28

Hodgkinson Rd

Nayland Rd

Culford Walk

Brandon Rd

Chelsworth Av

Kersey Rd

Ferry Ln

Waldgate Road

Vicarage Road

Mill Lane

Yeoman Road

Felixstowe RFC

Stour Av

Deben Wy

Butley Rd

Lincoln Ter

UNDERCLIFF

Oysterage

Wesel Avenue

Coronation

Elizabeth Way

Philip

Chaucer Rd

ORWELL RD

WEST

Riby Rd

Bacton Rd

Victor

NORWICH RD

1 grid square represents 500 metres

F G H J K

I

Felixstowe
Marsh

31 32

37

Marsh Lane

Rue's Farm

Gulpher

2

Gulpher Road

Rue's Lane

Fleet House

Gulpher Road

3

Park Farm

Hyem's Lane

Swallow Close

Conway Close

Brinkley Way

Ferry Road

Westmorland Road

Bawdsey Close

Eastcliff Av

Cliff Road

Felixstowe Ferry Golf Club

P

Suffolk Coast & Heaths Pth

Estuary Drive

Hollybush Dr

Eimcroft Lane

Ferry Road

Drive

Kings/Fleet Primary School

Western Road

Rydal Av

The Pines

36

Upperfield

Colneis Road

Colneis Junior School

St George's Road

Keswick Close

Castle

Roman Way

Dukes Close

4

Links Avenue

Rosemary Road

Sunningdale Drive

Went worth Dr

Gosford Way

Church Road

Old Felixstowe

Western Avenue

A1021

GROVE ROAD

BEATRICE AV

Dellwood Avenue

Fleetwood

Sunray Av

Prestwick Avenue

Ferndown Dr

Looe Quinton's

Carol

PO

Cliff Road

Golf Road

Marcus Road

5

Police Station

Fire Stn

West

Fairfield Infant Sch

Felixstowe & Walton FC

Lynwood Avenue

Felixstowe General Hospital

Elizabeth Orwell Hotel

High Road

Park Avenue

East

The Brackenbury Sports Centre

Maybush Lane

Martello

Gt Eastern Square

Card Cen

Surg

HAMILTON RD A1021

Croutel Road

Brook Road

Allenby Park

Picketts Road

Foxgrove

Thorney Rd

College of

Andrew's Road

Cowley Rd

Penfold

Palace

Gainsborough Rd

York Rd

Constable Road

Quilter Road

Rosebery Rd

Lane

Felixstowe College

Berners East

Beach East

Undercliff Road East

6

LEOPOLD RD

CRESCENT RD

HIGHFIELD

HAMILTON RD B1082

Victoria Street

Ranelagh Rd

Felixstowe General Hospital

Bath Road

Montague Rd

Cobbold Road

Bartlet Hospital

Barton Road

Bath Hill

The Cts

High Beach

Suffolk Coast & Heaths Path

2 35

F

BENT HL

PO

P

53

Spa Pavilion Theatre

Hamilton Gdns

Spa Gardens

31

G

H

J

K

32

Town Hall

B1082

FELIXSTOWE

HOLLY
BUSH
CORNER

A **B** B1068 **C** **D** **E**

Higham
Lodge

36 **04** 05 Wheatland
Farm 06 IPSWICH ROAD

I

Green Lane

Stratford
Hills

2

Hill
House

35

Higham Road

Lowe
Hill House

Billy's

Lane

School Lane

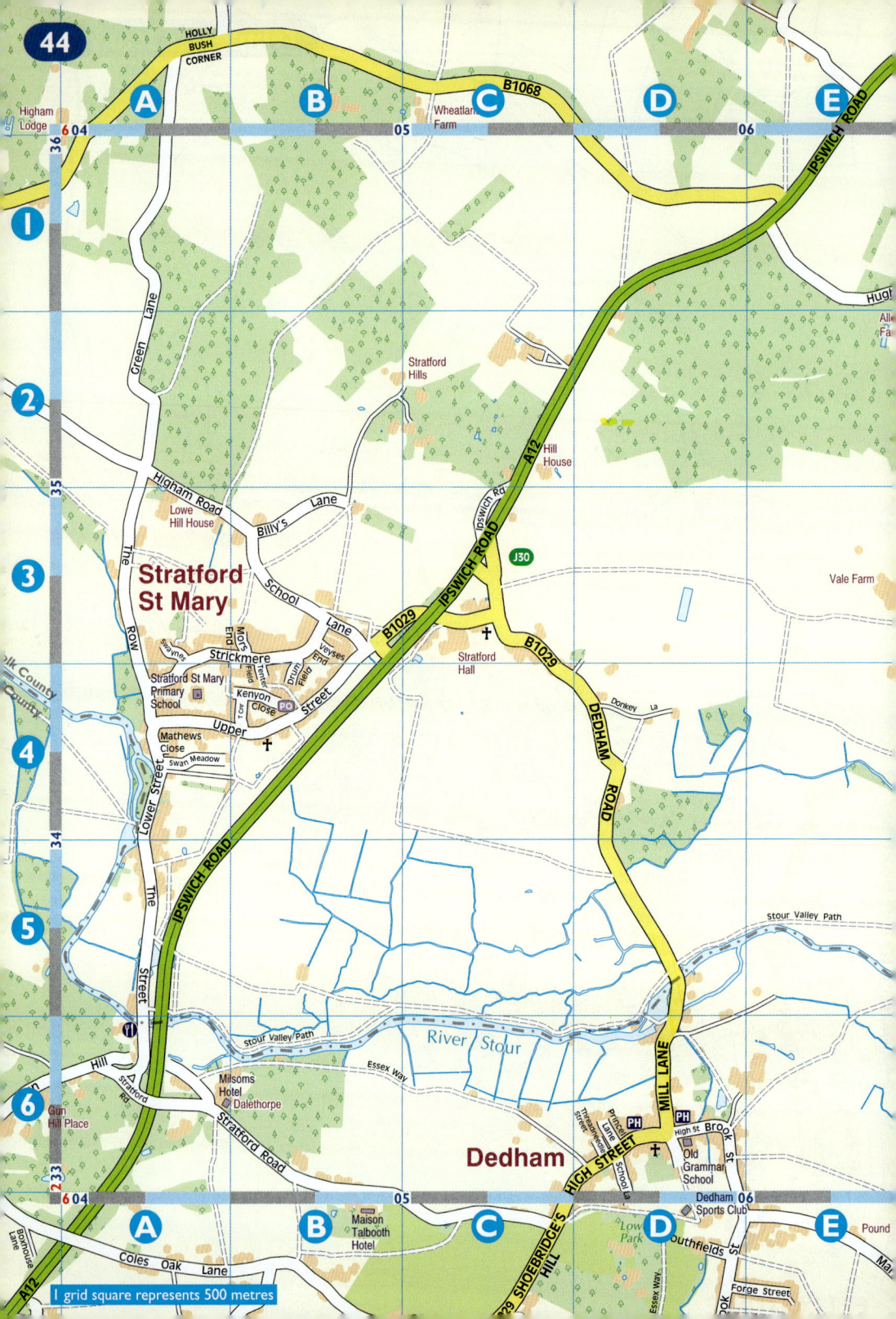

**Stratford
St Mary**

J30

3

The Row

Mol's
End

Veyses
End

Tenter
Field

B1029

IPSWICH ROAD

IPSWICH Rd

A12

Strickmere

Stratford
Hall

Stratford St Mary
Primary School

Swaynes

Drum
Field

Kenyon
Close

Upper

Street

PO

B1029

Vale Farm

Donkey La

DEDHAM ROAD

4

Mathews
Close

Swan Meadow

Suffolk County

County

Lower Street

34

5

Stour Valley Path

IPSWICH ROAD

Stour Valley Path

Essex Way

River Stour

MILL LANE

Stour Valley Path

The Street

Stratford Rd

Milsoms
Hotel

Dalethorpe

6

Gun
Hill Place

Hill

Stratford Road

PH

PH

High St

Brook St

Dedham
Sports Club

Princel
Lane

School La

Dedham

HIGH STREET

Old
Grammar
School

Dedham 06

Bownoux Lane

2 33

6 **04**

A12

A Coles Oak Lane **B** Maison
Talbooth
Hotel 05 **C** SHOEBRIDGES HILL **D** Southfields Low
Park Essex Way Cook St Forge Street **E** Pound
Mill

J31

F G Woodgates Farm H 38 J K

07 08 Cutlers Lane 09 36

I

East Bergholt

Woodgates Road

Barn Business Centre

Rookery Farm

East Bergholt High School

Collinswood Fields

Foxhall

Fiddlers Lane

Fordall Fields

Whites Field

Beehive Cl

GASTON END

Quintons Road

B1070 HEATH ROAD

Putticks Lane

2

Chaplin Road

Green Heath Close

Carters Ct

35

East End

Chaplin Road

Richardson

Potts End Road

Elm Lane

Hadleigh

Schools

East Bergholt Primary School

Askins Road

Gandish Close

Street

MILL

Highlands

3

Ackworth House

46

Road

HOP MEADOW

Gaston

Gandish Road

ROAD

Cemetery

4

PO

Cemetery Lane

The Street

Rectory Hill

Old Hall

White Horse Road

Notcutts

Orvis Lane

Cordwinders

MANNINGTREE

34

Fenbridge Lane

Flatford Road

Clapper Farm

Weirs Pond

Orvis Farm

Dazeley's Lane

5

Fen Bridge

Flatford Road

Stour Valley Path

Flatford Mill

Stour Valley Path

6

St Edmund Way

Flatford Bridge Cottage (NT)

2 33

07 08 09

F Suffolk County G H J K

Essex County

St Edmund Way

A B C **39** D E

10 11

I

Dodnash
Wood

Martins
Glen

Dodnash
Priory
Farm

The Grange

2

Fisher's Lane

Mission
La

East

East End Road

35

Park

End

Lane

Broom Knol

3

Park
House

Road

The
Drift

Slough

East End

Road

The
Poplars

Gravel

45

IPSWICH

Brantham

A137

School La

Church

Brantham
Glebe

Rectory La

4

Birch

Drive

Cedar

Sycamore

PO

Pine Ci

Way

Brooklands

Brooklands
Prim Sch

5

GTREE

34

Braham
Hall

BRANTHAM

HILL

Rise

Brooklands
Rd

Pattern Bush

Palfrey Hts

Road

Merriam
Ci

ROAD

Works

6

233
609

B1070 BERGHOLT ROAD

Brooklands

Cattawade St

Cattawade

Brantham
Athletic &
Social Club

Temple B Rd

Grimwade

Lane

Factory

Works

A B C D E

10 11

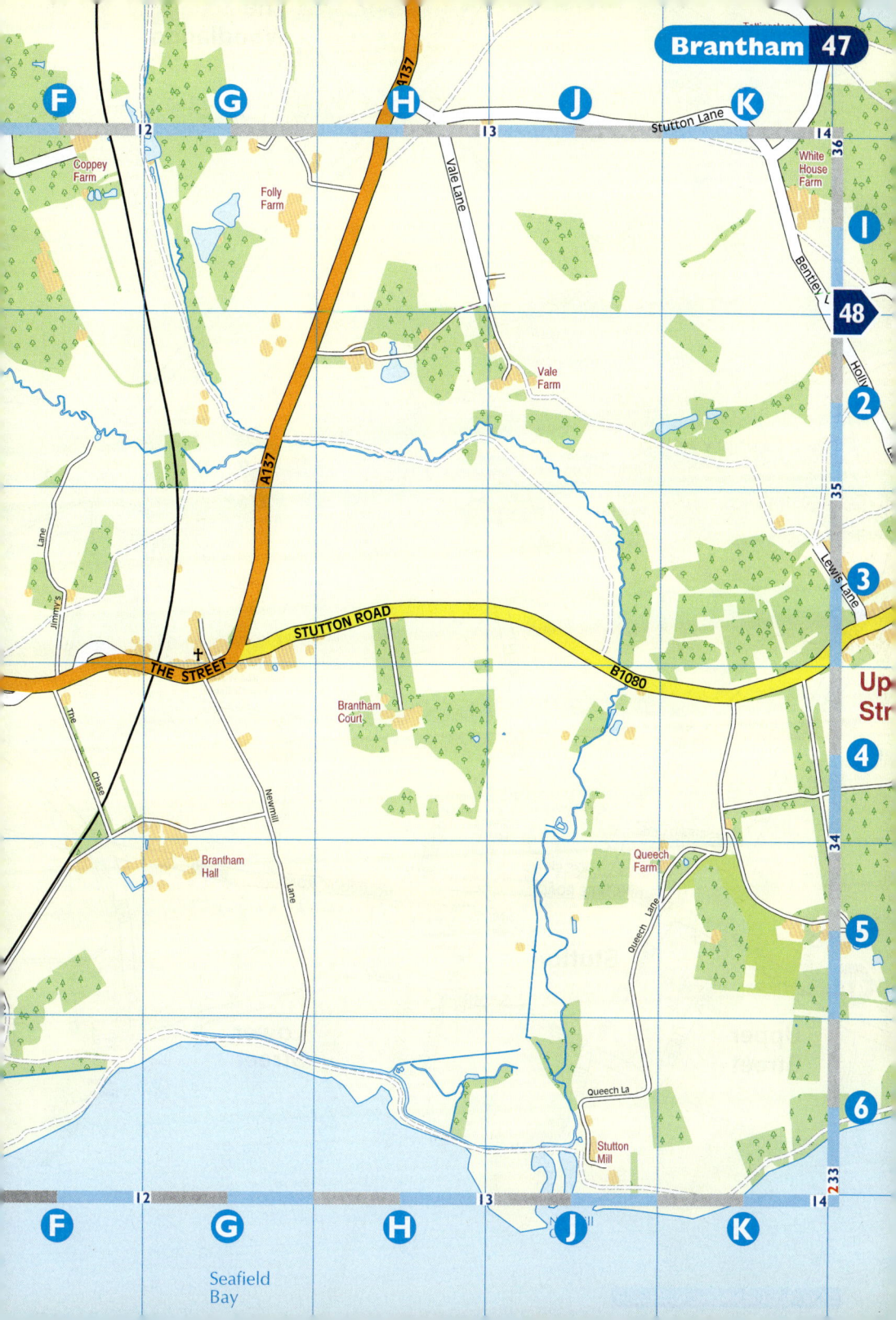

F
G
H
J
K

12
13
Stutton Lane
14

Coppey Farm

Folly Farm

White House Farm

36

I

48

Vale Lane

2

A137

35

Vale Farm

Lane

Jimmy's

3

Lewis Lane

STUTTON ROAD

B1080

Up
Str

THE STREET

Brantham Court

4

34

The Chase

Newmill

Queech Farm

Brantham Hall

Lane

Queech Lane

5

6

Queech La

Stutton Mill

2 33

F
G
H
J
K

12
13
14

Seafield Bay

A B C D E

I

Alton Water
(Reservoir)

The Woodlands

Bro
Far

IP

Hyams

2

White
House
Farm

Argent
Manor Farm

Alton Water
Sports Centre

3

Bentley Lane

4

Holly Lane

Bentley Lane

Woodfield Lane

Alton Hall Lane

Larksfield Rd

Catts
Cl
Cattsfield

Church Rd

MANNINGTREE ROAD

HOLBROOK ROAD

B1080

The Drift

5

Lewis Lane

Crepping Hall Drive

Manor Lane

Findley
Close

Church Road

Stutton CE
Primary
School

Stutton Cl

Lower

Street

Suffolk CC

Stutton Grn

47

Stutton

Upper
Street

Hyam's
La

Hyam's Lane

Crowe Hall Lane

Lower
Street

Stutton
House

6

Crepping
Hall

Crowe
Hall

A B C D E

1 grid square represents 500 metres

F G H J K

I

40

2

3

4

5

6

37 36 35 2 3 4

Road

Clench Rd

Close

IPSWICH ROAD

Holbrook High School

Holbrook CP School

Denmark Gdns

Coachman's Paddock

Street

Clifton Vw

Farm La

Gifford Close

Reade Road

Heathfield Road

PO

PH

B1080

Holbrook

CHURCH HILL

Five Acres

Mill Vw

Jervis Close

Little Orch

Fishponds Lane

Back   Hill

Fir Tree Hill

New Lane

PRIMROSE   HILL

Harkstead Lane

Holbrook Gardens

Brick Kiln Road

Red House Farm

Ipswich Road

The Vale Farm

Harkstead Road

Holbrook Lodge

Wardmaster Infirmary

Hospital

Lower Holbrook

Slushy Lane

Church

River Vw Road

Harkste

The Street

Walnut Tree La

Holbrook Rd

Shore Lane

Suffolk Coast & Heaths Path

Holbrook Creek

Suffolk Coast & Heaths Path

17 18 19

F G H J K

Holbrook Bay

A B **41** C D E

22 23

I

rence Park
Farm

2

35

3

PH **Erwarton**

The Street

Church Lane

**Shop
Corner**

Ness Road

4

34

Ness Farm

Suffolk Coast & Heaths Path

5

Suffolk Coast & Heaths Path

Erwarton Bay

6

2 33
22 23

A B C D E

Farm

Boot Drift

Shotley Hall

Church Walk

B1456

Warren Lane

Erwarton Walk

Shotley

THE STREET

PO

Surgery

Kingsland

Kingsland Queensland

Queensland

Suffolk County
Essex County

Stour

1 grid square represents 500 metres

hurch
nd

F · Frogs Alley

G

H

J

K

24

25

26

36

Trimle Marsh

Oldhall Road

1

I View Road

2

35

Shotley Primary School

Over Hall

Shotley Marshes

3

B1456

4

Childers Cl

Gate Farm Road

Great Harlings

Link Rd

Tudor Cl

34

Kirkton Cl

Blake Av

Stourside

Helena Rd

Kitchener Way

Shotley Gate

Ganges Museum

Marina

52

Stourside

Lloyd Rd

Ganges

Harlings

Lower

Estuary Cfs

Caledonia Rd

5

Estuary Road

BRISTOL HILL

PO

Battery Lane

Shotley Hill Park

School

6

Qu Victoria Dr

Shotley Sailing Club

King Edward Vll Drive

Suffolk County
Essex County

24

25

26

33

F

G

H

J

K

Pier at ch Hotel

Passenger Ferry Terminal

Harwich International Port Station

THE QUAY

King's Head

Works

Electr Palace

A · B · C · D **42** E

6 26 · 27 · 28

I

34

51

2

Oysterbed Road

Blofield Rd

A14

Parker Avenue

Falbury Road

Oysterbed Road

TRINITY AVENUE A154

Hodgkinson Rd

Euston

Bra

Ferry

Dooley Rd

Trinity Av

LC

Works

Bryon Av

Dyke Road

WALTON AVENUE

Cold Stor

3

The Port of Felixstowe

Harwich Harbour

33

Pier Road

Landguard Point

THE QUAY

Works

Electric Palace

Harwich Town Sailing Club

King's Quay St

Angelgate

WEST ST

GEORGE ST

PO

Guildhall

GEORGE ST

Admiral St

Pepys St

West St

St Helen's

Coke St

Harwich Town Station

Harwich Redoubt Fort

Harwich Prim Sch

Mayflower Av

HARBOUR CRESCENT

MAIN ROAD

Fernlea Rd

Mansitart St

Henning St

Alexandra Rd

Barrack La

Beacon

B1352

LC

HIGH

Hay Hall Theatre

Esplanade

Harwich Community Primary School

HARWICH

4

George St

5

32

6

P

Landguard Fort

Suffolk County / Essex County

6 26 · 27 · 28

A · B · C · D · E

ure erve

Landguard Point

Superstore

Grange Primary School

Surg

Cemetery

Playing Field

High School

Newry Av

Coyfield Avenue

Princes Rd

Crescent Rd

Cobbold

York Rd

Bath Hill

F   G   H   J   43   K

Felixstowe RFC

Yeoman Road

Grange Road

Oak Av

Waddate Road

Vicarage Road

Mill Lane

Thorn Way

Stour Av

Deben Wy

Chaucer Rd

Kings Fleet Rd

Butler Rd

Waveley Rd

St Johns Court

A1021

ORWELL RD

Garfield Rd

Bacton Rd

Ranby Rd

Victoria Rd

Queens Rd

Wolsey Gdns

Town Hall

B1082

Leopold C

Hamilton Gdns

Undercliff Rd W

Spa Pavilion Theatre

Suffolk Coast & Heaths Path

Coronation Drive

Charles Rd

Elizabeth Way

Andrew Close

Lincoln Ter

UNDERCLIFF RD WEST

Cavendish Road

Granville Road

Leisure Cen

FELIXSTOWE

Felixstowe Pier

Philip Avenue

Peewit Hill

Dovedale

Newbourne Gardens

Clopgrey Gdns

Langer Park Industrial Est

Holland Rd

Russell Rd

Beach Rd W

Buregate

Arwela Rd

Manwick Rd

Manning Road

Marlborough Hotel

Peewit Caravan Park

LANGER ROAD

A154

Langer Primary School

St Edmund's Road

Platters Rd

Micklegate

Marina Gdns

Sea Rd

A154

WALTON AV

LC STATION BEACH

Sub-Station

Haulters Road

Levington Rd

Orford Road

Tacon Rd

Orford Rd

Beach Station

Pretyman Road

Suffolk Coast & Heaths Path

CARR ROAD

A154

Manor Rd

Sunderland Rd

schneider cl

Adastra Close

Manor Terrace

View Point Road

F   29   G   30   H   J   31   K

I   1   2   3   4   5   6

31   34   33   232

Akenham	11	J5
Badley Hill	6	C3
Beacon Hill	20	E2
Belstead	31	F2
Bentley	39	J4
Blacksmith's Corner	31	F3
Bramford	16	D3
Brantham	46	D4
Brightwell	27	K4
Broke Hall	25	H4
Bucklesham	35	J1
Burgh	13	K1
California	25	G1
Campsea Ashe	9	H3
Capel St Mary	38	D1
Castle Hill	17	K2
Cattawade	46	D6
Chantry	23	H4
Chelmondiston	40	D4
Church End	41	K6
Claydon	11	F2
Coddenham Green	7	K3
Combs Ford	5	F5
The Common	10	C4
Copdock	30	C2
Culpho	12	E6
Dedham	44	C6
East Bergholt	45	G1
East End	46	D3
Erwarton	50	B3
Falkenham	37	G3
Falkenham Sink	37	J3
Felixstowe	53	J1
Freston	32	D6
Gainsborough	33	G1
Gipsy Row	38	B1
Great Bealings	13	K6
Great Blakenham	10	C2
Greenwich	24	C6
Grundisburgh	13	J3
Hadleigh	29	F4
Harkstead	49	K5
Harwich	52	A6
Hasketon	14	D1
Holbrook	49	G1
Ipswich	3	F6
Kesgrave	20	C6
Kirton	36	E2
Lattinford Hill	38	B5
Levington	35	F6
Little Bealings	20	E1
Little Blakenham	10	A5
Lower Falkenham	37	H4
Lower Hacheston	9	F1
Lower Holbrook	49	J4
Lower Street	48	D6
Mace Green	30	A2
Maidenhall	24	A5
Maidensgrave	15	F6
Martlesham	21	H3
Martlesham Heath	27	H1
Melton	15	J2
Mill Hills	15	H3
Nacton	34	D4
Needham Market	6	E4
Old Felixstowe	43	J5
Pettistree	8	C5
Pin Mill	40	D2
Playford	20	C1
The Port of Felixstowe	52	C3
Potash	39	J4
Priory Heath	25	J6
Racecourse	24	E5
Rose Hill	24	E3
Rushmere St Andrew	19	J5
Rushmere Street	20	A
Shop Corner	50	E
Shotley	50	E
Shotley Gate	51	H
Sproughton	22	E
Stoke	2	C
Stoke Park	23	E
Stowmarket	4	C
Stratford St Mary	44	A
Stutton	48	E
Thorpe Common	36	E
Trimley St Martin	36	C
Trimley St Mary	42	A
Upper Street	48	A
Walton	42	E
Warren Heath	26	A
Washbrook	22	E
Washbrook Street	22	E
Westbourne	17	H
Westerfield	18	C
Wherstead	32	A
White House	17	H
Whitton	17	C
Wickham Market	8	C
Woodbridge	15	E

USING THE STREET INDEX

Street names are listed alphabetically. Each street name is followed by its postal town or area locality, the Postcode District, the page number, and the reference to the square in which the name is found.

Standard index entries are shown as follows:

Abbey Gdns *FRAM/WMKT* IP13.......**9** J3

Street names and selected addresses not shown on the map due to scale restrictions are shown in the index with an asterisk:

Alafin Vls *MGTR* CO11 * **46** D5

GENERAL ABBREVIATIONS

ACC	ACCESS	E	EAST	LDG	LODGE	R	RIVE
ALY	ALLEY	EMB	EMBANKMENT	LGT	LIGHT	RBT	ROUNDABO
AP	APPROACH	EMBY	EMBASSY	LK	LOCK	RD	ROA
AR	ARCADE	ESP	ESPLANADE	LKS	LAKES	RDG	RIDC
ASS	ASSOCIATION	EST	ESTATE	LNDG	LANDING	REP	REPUBL
AV	AVENUE	EX	EXCHANGE	LTL	LITTLE	RES	RESERVO
BCH	BEACH	EXPY	EXPRESSWAY	LWR	LOWER	RFC	RUGBY FOOTBALL CLL
BLDS	BUILDINGS	EXT	EXTENSION	MAG	MAGISTRATES'	RI	RI
BND	BEND	F/O	FLYOVER	MAN	MANSIONS	RP	RAM
BNK	BANK	FC	FOOTBALL CLUB	MD	MEAD	RW	RO
BR	BRIDGE	FK	FORK	MDW	MEADOWS	S	SOU
BRK	BROOK	FLD	FIELD	MEM	MEMORIAL	SCH	SCHO(
BTM	BOTTOM	FLDS	FIELDS	MI	MILL	SE	SOUTH EA
BUS	BUSINESS	FLS	FALLS	MKT	MARKET	SER	SERVICE ARE
BVD	BOULEVARD	FM	FARM	MKTS	MARKETS	SH	SHO
BY	BYPASS	FT	FORT	ML	MALL	SHOP	SHOPPIN
CATH	CATHEDRAL	FTS	FLATS	MNR	MANOR	SKWY	SKYW
CEM	CEMETERY	FWY	FREEWAY	MS	MEWS	SMT	SUMM
CEN	CENTRE	FY	FERRY	MSN	MISSION	SOC	SOCIE
CFT	CROFT	GA	GATE	MT	MOUNT	SP	SPL
CH	CHURCH	GAL	GALLERY	MTN	MOUNTAIN	SPR	SPRIN
CHA	CHASE	GDN	GARDEN	MTS	MOUNTAINS	SQ	SQUA
CHYD	CHURCHYARD	GDNS	GARDENS	MUS	MUSEUM	ST	STRE
CIR	CIRCLE	GLD	GLADE	MWY	MOTORWAY	STN	STATIC
CIRC	CIRCUS	GLN	GLEN	N	NORTH	STR	STREA
CL	CLOSE	GN	GREEN	NE	NORTH EAST	STRD	STRAN
CLFS	CLIFFS	GND	GROUND	NW	NORTH WEST	SW	SOUTH WE
CMP	CAMP	GRA	GRANGE	O/P	OVERPASS	TDG	TRADI
CNR	CORNER	GRG	GARAGE	OFF	OFFICE	TER	TERRA
CO	COUNTY	GT	GREAT	ORCH	ORCHARD	THWY	THROUGHW
COLL	COLLEGE	GTWY	GATEWAY	OV	OVAL	TNL	TUNN
COM	COMMON	GV	GROVE	PAL	PALACE	TOLL	TOLLW
COMM	COMMISSION	HGR	HIGHER	PAS	PASSAGE	TPK	TURNPI
CON	CONVENT	HL	HILL	PAV	PAVILION	TR	TRA
COT	COTTAGE	HLS	HILLS	PDE	PARADE	TRL	TRA
COTS	COTTAGES	HO	HOUSE	PH	PUBLIC HOUSE	TWR	TOW
CP	CAPE	HOL	HOLLOW	PK	PARK	U/P	UNDERPA
CPS	COPSE	HOSP	HOSPITAL	PKWY	PARKWAY	UNI	UNIVERSI
CR	CREEK	HRB	HARBOUR	PL	PLACE	UPR	UPP
CREM	CREMATORIUM	HTH	HEATH	PLN	PLAIN	V	VA
CRS	CRESCENT	HTS	HEIGHTS	PLNS	PLAINS	VA	VALL
CSWY	CAUSEWAY	HVN	HAVEN	PLZ	PLAZA	VIAD	VIADU
CT	COURT	HWY	HIGHWAY	POL	POLICE STATION	VIL	VIL
CTRL	CENTRAL	IMP	IMPERIAL	PR	PRINCE	VIS	VIS
CTS	COURTS	IN	INLET	PREC	PRECINCT	VLG	VILLA
CTYD	COURTYARD	IND EST	INDUSTRIAL ESTATE	PREP	PREPARATORY	VLS	VILL
CUTT	CUTTINGS	INF	INFIRMARY	PRIM	PRIMARY	VW	VIE
CV	COVE	INFO	INFORMATION	PROM	PROMENADE	W	WE
CYN	CANYON	INT	INTERCHANGE	PRS	PRINCESS	WD	WO
DEPT	DEPARTMENT	IS	ISLAND	PRT	PORT	WHF	WHA
DL	DALE	JCT	JUNCTION	PT	POINT	WK	WA
DM	DAM	JTY	JETTY	PTH	PATH	WKS	WAI
DR	DRIVE	KG	KING	PZ	PIAZZA	WLS	WEI
DRO	DROVE	KNL	KNOLL	QD	QUADRANT	WY	W
DRY	DRIVEWAY	L	LAKE	QU	QUEEN	YD	YA
DWGS	DWELLINGS	LA	LANE	QY	QUAY	YHA	YOUTH HOST

POSTCODE TOWNS AND AREA ABBREVIATIONS

CHTY .... Chantry
FRAM/WMKT ....Framlingham/Wickham Market
FX ....Felixstowe
HADL ....Hadleigh

HAR ....Harwich
IP ....Ipswich
IPNE ....Ipswich northeast
IPSE ....Ipswich southeast
KESG ....Kesgrave

KIR/NAC .... Kirton/Nacton
MGTR .... Manningtree
NHMKT .... Needham Market
RCOLE ......Rural Colchester east

RIPS/CAP ....Rural Ipswich south/Capel St Mary
RIPW .... Rural Ipswich west
SMKT .... Stowmarket
WDBR .... Woodbridge

Index - streets

Abb - Boy

A

Abbey Gdns FRAM/WMKT IP13.......9 J3
Abbotsbury Cl CHTY IP2 ....23 K6
Abbot's Hall Rd SMKT IP14.........4 E4
Aberdare Cl CHTY IP2 ....24 A5
Aberdeen Wy IPNE IP4..............19 H4
Aberfoyle Cl IPNE IP4................19 H4
Ablitts Meadow
    FRAM/WMKT IP13..................13 H2
Acacia Cl IPSE IP3.....................25 K6
Acer Gv RIPW IP8........................23 F6
Acorn Cl CHTY IP2.....................23 F5
Acorn Wy KESG IP5....................21 K5
Acton Cl RIPW IP8......................16 D3
Acton Gdns RIPW IP8.................16 D3
Acton Rd RIPW IP8.....................16 D3
Adair Rd IP IP1..........................17 G5
Adams Cl CHTY IP2....................24 B4
Adams Pl KESG IP5.....................20 D6
Adastral Cl FX IP11......................53 F4
Addington Rd FX IP11.................42 B3
Addison Wy NHMKT IP6.............10 D3
Adelaide Rd IPNE IP4.................25 J1
Admiral Rd RIPW IP8..................31 H1
Agate Cl IP IP1...........................17 G4
Ainslie Rd IP IP1..........................2 A2
Aisthorpe RIPS/CAP IP9.............38 D2
Alan Rd IPSE IP3.........................24 E3
Alban Sq WDBR IP12..................21 J3
The Albany IPNE IP4..................18 D5
Alberta Cl KESG IP5....................20 B5
Albion Hl IPNE IP4........................3 K1
Aldercroft Cl IP IP1.....................18 A2
Aldercroft Rd IP IP1...................18 A3
Alderlee CHTY IP2......................31 J1
Alderman Rd IP IP1.......................2 B3
Aldham Gdns SMKT IP14.............5 F5
Aldham Mill Hl HADL IP7............28 E2
Aldham Rd HADL IP7..................29 F3
Aldis Av SMKT IP14.....................5 H1
Aldous Cl RCOLE CO7.................45 G2
Aldringham Ms FX IP11..............42 C5
Alexandra Rd FX IP11.................42 D4
Alexandra Rd FX IP11.................42 D4
Alice Driver Rd
    FRAM/WMKT IP13..................13 H3
Allenby Rd CHTY IP2..................23 J1
Allen Rd HADL IP7......................28 E3
Alley Rd KIR/NAC IP10................36 E3
Allington Cl IPNE IP4..................18 E6
All Saints' Rd IP IP1....................17 K6
All Saints Rd NHMKT IP6..............7 G1
Alma Cl IPNE IP4........................19 F4
Almondhayes CHTY IP2..............24 A4
Alnesbourn Crs IPSE IP3.............33 J2
Alpe St IP IP1................................2 B1
Alston Rd IPSE IP3.....................24 E3
Alton Hall La RIPS/CAP IP9.........48 D3
Ancaster Rd CHTY IP2..................2 B7
Anchor St IPSE IP3.......................3 H7
Anderson Cl NHMKT IP6..............6 D4
Anderson's Wy WDBR IP12.........15 F5
Andrew Cl FX IP11......................53 G1
Andros Cl IPSE IP3......................33 F2
Angela Cl WDBR IP12.................21 J3
Angelgate HAR CO12 *...............52 A4
Angel Ga HAR CO12 *.................52 A4
Angel La IPNE IP4........................3 G5
    WDBR IP12.............................15 G4
Angel Rd RIPW IP8......................16 D3
Angel St HADL IP7.......................28 E4
Anglesea Rd IP IP1.......................2 C1
Anglia Pkwy North IP IP1............17 G1
Anglia Pkwy South IP IP1............17 G1
Angus Cl IPNE IP4......................19 G4
Anita Cl East CHTY IP2................23 H2
Anita Cl West CHTY IP2...............23 H2

Ann Beaumont Wy HADL IP7.......28 D3
Annbrook Rd CHTY IP2...............23 H6
Anne Cl FX IP11..........................53 G1
Anni Healey Cl WDBR IP12.........15 C3
Ann St IP IP1.................................2 B1
Ansell Cl HADL IP7.....................28 E4
Anson Rd KESG IP5.....................21 J5
Antrim Rd IP IP1.........................17 G4
Anzani Av FX IP11.......................42 B6
Appleby Cl CHTY IP2..................23 F6
Arcade St IP IP1............................2 D3
Archangel Gdns CHTY IP2 *........23 H3
The Arches WDBR IP12 *............15 H4
Argyle St IPNE IP4.........................3 G3
Arkle Ct KESG IP5.......................20 E6
Arnold Cl IP IP1..........................17 J2
Arthurs Ter IPNE IP4.....................3 G2
Arundel Wy IPSE IP3...................25 K4
Arwela Rd FX IP11......................53 H2
Ascot Dr FX IP11........................42 D4
    IPSE IP3.................................25 G4
Ashburnham Rd NHMKT IP6.........6 D5
Ash Cl IPSE IP3...........................26 A6
    WDBR IP12.............................15 C5
Ashcroft Rd IP IP1.......................17 J4
Ashdale Rd KESG IP5..................20 E5
Ashdown Wy IPSE IP3.................25 J4
Ash Ground Cl FX IP11................36 E6
    MGTR CO11............................46 D5
Ash Gv RIPS/CAP IP9.................38 E2
Ashley St CHTY IP2.......................2 E7
Ashmere Gv IPNE IP4...................3 K2
Ash Rd FRAM/WMKT IP13............8 E2
Ashton Cl CHTY IP2.....................23 F5
Askins Rd RCOLE CO7.................45 C2
Aspen Cl NHMKT IP6...................10 C1
    WDBR IP12.............................15 J3
Aster Rd CHTY IP2.......................23 H3
Ataka Rd FX IP11........................42 E4
Athenrye Ct WDBR IP12 *...........15 H5
Atherton Rd CHTY IP2.................23 G5
Audley Gv IPNE IP4.....................26 A2
Austin St CHTY IP2.......................2 E6
The Avenue FX IP11....................42 A3
    IP IP1....................................18 B4
    KESG IP5................................21 K5
    RIPW IP8................................30 C2
    WDBR IP12.............................15 H5
Avocet Ct FX IP11 *....................53 H2
Avocet Gdns SMKT IP14...............5 C3
Avocet La KESG IP5....................21 H6
Avondale Rd IPSE IP3.................25 F5
Aylward Cl HADL IP7...................29 F6
Ayr Rd IPNE IP4..........................19 G4

B

Back Hamlet IPSE IP3....................3 H5
Back Hl RIPS/CAP IP9.................49 G3
Back La FX IP11..........................42 E5
    KIR/NAC IP10.........................37 H4
    NHMKT IP6.............................11 F3
    RIPW IP8................................30 B1
Back Rd KIR/NAC IP10................36 E3
Bacon Rd NHMKT IP6..................11 F2
Bacton Rd FX IP11......................53 H1
Bader Cl IPSE IP3........................25 H5
Bader Ct KESG IP5......................21 H6
Badgers Bank CHTY IP2..............23 H6
Badley Hl NHMKT IP6...................6 C2
Badley Wk NHMKT IP6.................6 B2
Badsham Av IPSE IP3..................25 G4
Bailey Av KESG IP5.....................21 F6
Bailey Cl CHTY IP2......................23 H1
Baird Cl CHTY IP2.......................17 J6
Baird Gv KESG IP5......................26 C1
Baker Rd RIPS/CAP IP9...............51 G5
Bakers La WDBR IP12 *...............15 H4
Baldry Cl RIPW IP8.....................23 F6
Baldwin Rd SMKT IP14.................4 D5
Ballater Cl IP IP1.........................17 H1

Balmoral Cl CHTY IP2.................23 J6
Bank Rd IPNE IP4..........................3 J2
Banks Cl HADL IP7......................29 F5
Bantoft Ter IPSE IP3....................25 H5
Banyard Cl KESG IP5..................20 E6
Barhams Wy FRAM/WMKT IP13.....8 D2
Barker Cl CHTY IP2.....................23 G2
Barking Rd NHMKT IP6.................6 E6
Barleyhayes Cl CHTY IP2............24 A5
Barnes Cl HADL IP7....................29 F4
Barnfield FX IP11........................42 C4
    RIPS/CAP IP9.........................39 F2
Barnham Pl KESG IP5..................26 A1
Barons Cl FX IP11.......................43 J4
Baronsdale Cl IP IP1...................18 A4
Barrack La HAR CO12..................52 A6
    IP IP1......................................2 C2
Barrack Sq KESG IP5..................21 J6
Barrett's La NHMKT IP6................6 C5
Bartholomew St IPNE IP4..............3 K3
Barton Cl CHTY IP2....................23 H5
    WDBR IP12.............................15 G2
Barton Rd FX IP11......................43 G6
Bath Hl FX IP11..........................43 G6
Bath Hl FX IP11..........................43 G6
Bath St CHTY IP2........................24 C4
Battery La RIPS/CAP IP9.............51 H5
Battles La KESG IP5....................20 E6
Bawdsey Cl FX IP11....................43 J3
Beach Rd East FX IP11................43 H6
Beach Rd West FX IP11...............53 H2
Beach Station Rd FX IP11............53 G2
Beacon Fld FX IP11.....................42 D5
Beacon Hill Av CHTY IP2.............52 A6
Beacon La FRAM/WMKT IP13.......21 G2
Beaconsfield Rd IP IP1................17 J6
    WDBR IP12.............................15 H4
Bealings La FRAM/WMKT IP13.....14 A3
Bealings Rd WDBR IP12..............21 J2
Beardmore Pk KESG IP5..............21 J5
Beatrice Av FX IP11....................43 F4
Beatrice Cl IPSE IP3....................25 F4
Beatty Rd IPSE IP3......................25 G5
Beaufort St IP IP1.........................2 A1
Beaumont Wy SMKT IP14..............4 C4
The Becketts SMKT IP14...............4 C1
Bedford St IP IP1...........................2 C2
Beech Cl RIPW IP8......................22 D1
Beechcroft Rd IP IP1...................17 J3
The Beeches IPSE IP3...................3 K6
    NHMKT IP6.............................11 F5
    RIPW IP8................................10 A5
Beech Gv IPSE IP3......................24 E4
    KESG IP5................................20 A6
Beech Rd KESG IP5.....................20 A6
Beech Ter SMKT IP14....................4 E2
Beech Wy WDBR IP12.................15 G6
Beehive Cl RCOLE CO7................45 G2
Belgrave Cl IPNE IP4..................18 D4
Bell Cl CHTY IP2...........................2 E6
Belle Vue Rd IPNE IP4...................3 J2
Bell La CHTY IP2...........................2 E6
    KESG IP5................................26 C2
Belmont Rd RIPW IP8..................23 F6
Belstead Av CHTY IP2.................24 A4
Belstead Rd CHTY IP2.................24 D7
Belvedere Rd IPNE IP4................18 E5
Benacre Rd IPSE IP3...................25 F5
Benezet St IP IP1..........................2 B1
Bennett Rd IP IP1.......................17 G5
Bent Hl FX IP11..........................53 J1
Bent La IPNE IP4.........................49 K5
Bentley La RIPS/CAP IP9.............47 K1
    RIPW IP8................................31 F4
Bentley Rd IP IP1........................17 F4
Benton St HADL IP7....................28 E4
Beresford Dr WDBR IP12.............15 G2
Bergholt Rd MGTR CO11.............46 B6
Berkeley Cl FX IP11.....................18 D4
Bermuda Rd IPSE IP3..................33 K2
Bernard Crs IPSE IP3...................25 F3
Berners Rd FX IP11.....................43 H6
Berners St IP IP1...........................2 C2
Berry Cl IPSE IP3.........................25 A6

Berry Rd IPSE IP3.......................34 A2
Betts Av KESG IP5.......................21 J6
Betts Cl HADL IP7.......................28 E3
Beverley Rd IPNE IP4..................18 E5
Bibb Wy IP IP1..............................2 A4
Bilberry Rd FX IP11.....................33 H2
Bildeston Gdns IP IP1.................18 C4
Billy's La RCOLE CO7..................44 B3
Bilney Rd WDBR IP12..................15 F4
Birch Cl FRAM/WMKT IP13............8 D3
    SMKT IP14...............................5 H1
    WDBR IP12.............................15 G6
Birchcroft Rd IP IP1....................18 A3
Birch Dr MGTR CO11..................46 D4
Birch Gv KESG IP5......................27 J1
Birchwood Dr KESG IP5..............19 K4
Birkfield Cl CHTY IP2..................23 K3
Birkfield Dr CHTY IP2..................23 H6
Bishops Cl FX IP11......................43 J4
Bishop's Hl IPSE IP3.....................3 J6
Bittern Cl CHTY IP2.....................23 H4
Bixley Dr IPNE IP4......................25 K2
Bixley La IPNE IP4......................26 A2
Bixley Rd IPSE IP3......................25 J4
Black Barns FX IP11....................42 B3
Blackbird Wy SMKT IP14...............5 H3
Blackdown Av KESG IP5..............26 A1
Blackfriars Ct IPNE IP4..................3 F4
Black Horse La IP IP1....................2 D3
Blacksmiths Rd
    FRAM/WMKT IP13..................14 D2
Blackthorn Cl IPSE IP3................25 K6
Blacktiles La WDBR IP12.............21 H3
Bladen Dr IPNE IP4.....................26 A2
Blair Cl IPNE IP4.........................25 K2
Blake Av RIPS/CAP IP9...............51 G4
Blake Rd IP IP1...........................17 J2
    SMKT IP14...............................4 C2
Blakes Cl WDBR IP12..................15 K2
Blanche St IPNE IP4......................3 G3
Blandford Rd IPSE IP3.................25 J4
Blenheim Cl MGTR CO11.............46 D4
Blenheim Rd IP IP1.....................17 K6
Blickling Cl CHTY IP2..................24 A5
Blofield Cl FX IP11......................42 B6
Bloomfield St IPNE IP4................25 G1
Blue Barn Cl FX IP11...................36 D6
Blue Barn La NHMKT IP6.............10 C3
Bluebell Cl CHTY IP2..................23 H3
Bluebell Gv NHMKT IP6................6 E6
Bluegate La RIPS/CAP IP9...........38 E4
Bluestem Rd IPSE IP3..................33 J1
Blyford Wy FX IP11.....................42 B6
Blyth Cl CHTY IP2.......................23 K6
Bobbits La RIPS/CAP IP9............31 J2
    RIPW IP8................................31 H1
Bodiam Cl IPSE IP3.....................25 J3
Bodiam Rd IPSE IP3....................25 J3
Bodmin Cl KESG IP5...................26 B1
Bolton La IPNE IP4........................3 F2
Bond St IPNE IP4...........................3 G4
    SMKT IP14...............................4 E2
Bonnington Rd IPSE IP3..............24 E6
Bonny Crs IPSE IP3.....................33 H1
Boot Drift RIPS/CAP IP9.............41 G6
Booth La KESG IP5......................21 F5
Border Cot La FRAM/WMKT IP13...8 D2
Borrett Pl WDBR IP12..................14 E6
Borrowdale Av IPNE IP4..............18 C4
Bosmere Ct NHMKT IP6 *..............6 E5
Boss Hall Rd IP IP1.....................17 G6
Bostock Rd CHTY IP2..................24 B6
Boston Rd IPNE IP4....................18 E6
Boswell La HADL IP7...................28 E3
Boulge Rd FRAM/WMKT IP13.......13 K1
Boulters Cl SMKT IP14..................4 C3
Boulters Wy SMKT IP14................4 C3
Bourchier Cl HADL IP7................29 F4
Bourne Hl CHTY IP2....................32 B1
Bowland Dr RIPW IP8..................23 F6
Bowthorpe Cl IP IP1...................17 H1
Boxford Cl SMKT IP14...................5 F6
Boxford Ct FX IP11.....................42 B6
Boydlands RIPS/CAP IP9.............38 E2

Boyton Rd *IPSE* IP3 .... 33 G1
Bracken Av *KESG* IP5 .... 21 F4
Brackenbury CI *IP* IP1 .... 18 A5
Brackenhayes CI *CHTY* IP2 .... 24 A4
Brackley CI *FX* IP11 .... 42 C5
Bradfield Av *HADL* IP7 .... 28 E3
Bradfield Crs *HADL* IP7 .... 28 E3
Bradley St *IP* IP2 .... 2 D7
Bramble Dr *IPSE* IP3 .... 25 K6
Bramblewood *RIPW* IP8 .... 23 F5
Brambling CI *SMKT* IP14 .... 5 H4
Bramford La *IP* IP1 .... 17 G4
Bramford Rd *IP* IP1 .... 17 F5
  NHMKT IP6 .... 10 C2
Bramhall CI *CHTY* IP2 .... 23 G6
Brandon Rd *FX* IP11 .... 42 B6
Bransby Gdns *IPNE* IP4 .... 3 H1
Brantham Hill *MGTR* CO11 ..... 46 C5
Brazier's Wood Rd *IPSE* IP3 .... 33 K3
Brecon CI *CHTY* IP2 .... 24 A5
Bredfield CI *FX* IP11 .... 42 C5
Bredfield Rd *WDBR* IP12 .... 15 G2
Bredfield St *WDBR* IP12 .... 15 G4
Brendon Dr *KESG* IP5 .... 26 A1
Brett Av *HADL* IP7 .... 29 F3
Brett CI *IP* IP1 .... 17 H5
Brettenham Crs *IP* IP1 .... 18 C4
The Bretts *KESG* IP5 .... 21 F5
Briarhayes CI *CHTY* IP2 .... 24 A4
Briarwood Rd *WDBR* IP12 ..... 15 F6
Brickfield CI *CHTY* IP2 .... 24 C4
The Brickfields *SMKT* IP14 .... 4 D3
Brickfield Ter *RIPS/CAP* IP9 * . 41 H5
Brick Kiln Cots *FX* IP11 * 43 F2
Brick Kiln Rd *RIPS/CAP* IP9 .... 49 K2
Bridge Rd *FX* IP11 .... 43 F5
  KIR/NAC IP10 .... 35 F6
Bridge St *HADL* IP7 .... 28 D4
  IP IP1 .... 2 E6
  NHMKT IP6 .... 6 E4
  SMKT IP14 .... 5 F4
Bridgewood Rd *WDBR* IP12 ... 15 F4
Bridgwater Rd *CHTY* IP2 .... 23 G5
Bridle Wy *IP* IP1 .... 18 B6
Bridport Av *IPSE* IP3 .... 25 J4
Brights Wk *KESG* IP5 .... 21 F6
Brightwell CI *FX* IP11 .... 42 B6
Brimstone Rd *RIPW* IP8 .... 31 H1
Brinkley Wy *FX* IP11 .... 43 J3
Brisbane Rd *IPNE* IP4 .... 25 J1
Bristol HI *RIPS/CAP* IP9 .... 51 H5
Bristol Hill Pk *RIPS/CAP* IP9 .. 51 H5
Bristol Rd *IPNE* IP4 .... 19 F6
Britannia Rd *IPNE* IP4 .... 25 G1
Britten Av *SMKT* IP14 .... 4 D2
Broadlands Wy *IPNE* IP4 .... 26 A2
Broad Meadow *RIPW* IP8 ...... 23 F5
Broadmere Rd *IP* IP1 .... 17 H5
Broad Rd *FRAM/WMKT* IP13 ..... 8 C2
Broadwater Gdns *RIPS/CAP* IP9 . 51 G5
Broadway *FRAM/WMKT* IP13 ..... 8 C2
Broadway La *IP* IP1 .... 17 H3
Brock La *WDBR* IP12 .... 21 K1
Brockley Crs *IP* IP1 .... 17 G4
Broke Av *RIPW* IP8 .... 16 E3
Broke Hall Gdns *IPSE* IP3 ...... 25 J3
Bromeswell Rd *IPNE* IP4 .... 18 D4
Bromley CI *CHTY* IP2 .... 24 B4
Brook CI *SMKT* IP14 .... 4 C2
Brook Farm La *RIPS/CAP* IP9 .. 48 E1
Brookfield Rd *IP* IP1 .... 17 J5
Brookhill Wy *SMKT* IP14 .... 26 A3
Brooklands Ri *MGTR* CO11 ..... 46 D5
Brooklands Rd *MGTR* CO11 .... 46 C6
Brook La *FX* IP11 .... 37 G6
  NHMKT IP6 .... 20 B1
  RIPS/CAP IP9 .... 38 C1
Brooks Hall Rd *IP* IP1 .... 17 K6
Brook St *RCOLE* CO7 .... 44 D6
  WDBR IP12 .... 15 H4
Brookview *RIPW* IP8 .... 23 H6
Broom Crs *IPSE* IP3 .... 24 E6
Broom Fld *FX* IP11 .... 42 D5
Broomfield *KESG* IP5 .... 21 G6
Broomfield Common *RIPW* IP8 . 22 E1
Broomfield Ms *KESG* IP5 .... 21 H6
Broomhayes *CHTY* IP2 .... 23 K5
Broomhill *RIPS/CAP* IP9 * 49 F1
Broom Hill Rd *IP* IP1 .... 17 K5
Broom Knoll *RCOLE* CO7 .... 46 D5
Broomspath Rd *SMKT* IP14 .... 5 H1
Broom Wy *RIPS/CAP* IP9 .... 38 E1
Brotherton Av *FX* IP11 .... 42 A2
Broughton Rd *IP* IP1 .... 18 A6
Browning Rd *IP* IP1 .... 17 J2
  MGTR CO11 .... 46 C6
Brownlow Rd *FX* IP11 .... 43 F6
Browns Gv *KESG* IP5 .... 20 E6
Bruff Rd *CHTY* IP2 .... 24 B4

Brunel Rd *CHTY* IP2 .... 23 H1
Brunskill PI *HADL* IP7 * 28 D3
Brunswick Rd *IPNE* IP4 .... 18 E6
Bryon Av *FX* IP11 .... 52 D1
Buckenham Rd *HADL* IP7 ...... 29 G6
Buckfast CI *FX* IP11 .... 23 K5
Buckingham CI *WDBR* IP12 ... 21 H3
Bucklesham Rd *IPSE* IP3 .... 25 J5
  KIR/NAC IP10 .... 36 E2
  KIR/NAC IP10 .... 27 F6
Buck's Head La *NHMKT* IP6 ...... 7 K3
Buck's Horns La *RIPW* IP8 ..... 30 E3
Buddleia CI *CHTY* IP2 .... 23 H5
Bude CI *KESG* IP5 .... 26 B1
Bugsby Wy *KESG* IP5 .... 21 F6
Bullard's La *WDBR* IP12 .... 15 F4
Bull Dr *KESG* IP5 .... 26 D1
Bullen CI *RIPW* IP8 .... 16 D3
Bullen La *RIPW* IP8 .... 16 C4
Bullfinch CI *SMKT* IP14 .... 5 G3
Bull Hall La *NHMKT* IP6 .... 12 A4
Bull Rd *IPSE* IP3 .... 25 G3
Bulls Cliff *FX* IP11 * 53 H1
  IP IP1 .... 2 A2
Bulstrode Rd *CHTY* IP2 .... 3 F6
Bulwer Rd *IP* IP1 .... 2 D5
The Bungalows *KIR/NAC* IP10 * . 34 C5
Bunting Rd *CHTY* IP2 .... 23 G4
The Buntings *SMKT* IP14 .... 5 J4
Bunyan CI *IP* IP1 .... 17 K2
Buregate Rd *FX* IP11 .... 53 H2
Bures CI *SMKT* IP14 .... 5 F5
Burgess PI *KESG* IP5 .... 21 J6
Burghley CI *CHTY* IP2 .... 23 K5
Burke CI *IP* IP1 .... 17 J2
Burke Rd *IP* IP1 .... 17 J2
Burkitt Rd *WDBR* IP12 .... 15 G4
Burlington Rd *IP* IP1 .... 2 B3
Burnet CI *RIPW* IP8 .... 31 G1
Burnham CI *FX* IP11 .... 42 B3
  IPNE IP4 .... 18 E6
Burns Rd *IP* IP1 .... 17 H2
Burnt House La *KIR/NAC* IP10 . 36 E2
Burrell Rd *CHTY* IP2 .... 2 C6
Burstall La *RIPW* IP8 .... 22 C1
Burton Dr *NHMKT* IP6 .... 6 D4
Burwood PI *FX* IP11 .... 42 B2
Bury HI *WDBR* IP12 .... 15 H2
Bury Hill CI *WDBR* IP12 .... 15 H2
Bury Rd *IP* IP1 .... 17 F1
  SMKT IP14 .... 4 E2
Bury St *SMKT* IP14 .... 4 E3
Bushey CI *RIPS/CAP* IP9 .... 38 E2
Bushman Gdns *RIPW* IP8 ...... 16 D3
Butchers La *RIPS/CAP* IP9 ..... 39 F2
Butler Smith Gdns *KESG* IP5 .. 20 D6
Butley CI *CHTY* IP2 .... 31 J1
Butley Rd *FX* IP11 .... 53 C1
Buttercup CI *RIPW* IP8 .... 23 F6
Butterfly Gdns *IPNE* IP4 .... 25 K2
Buttermarket *IP* IP1 .... 2 E3
Bylam La *RIPS/CAP* IP9 .... 40 A4
Byland CI *CHTY* IP2 .... 23 K5
Byng La *FRAM/WMKT* IP13 ...... 8 A6
Byron Rd *IP* IP1 .... 17 H1

C

Cage La *FX* IP11 .... 42 D5
Caithness CI *IPNE* IP4 .... 19 G5
Calais St *HADL* IP7 .... 28 E4
Caledonia Rd *RIPS/CAP* IP9 ... 51 H5
California *WDBR* IP12 .... 14 E6
Callisto Ct *IP* IP1 .... 17 G6
Camberley Rd *IPNE* IP4 .... 19 J6
Camborne Rd *KESG* IP5 .... 26 C1
Cambridge Dr *CHTY* IP2 .... 23 H6
Cambridge Rd *FX* IP11 .... 43 G6
  KESG IP5 .... 20 B5
Camden La *IPSE* IP3 .... 25 C3
Campbell Rd *IPSE* IP3 .... 25 H6
Campion Crs *SMKT* IP14 .... 4 D5
Campion Rd *CHTY* IP2 .... 23 J3
Camwood Gdns *IPSE* IP3 .... 25 G3
Canberra CI *IPNE* IP4 .... 25 J1
Candlet Gv *FX* IP11 .... 42 E5
Candlet Rd *FX* IP11 .... 42 D3
Canham St *IP* IP1 .... 2 C3
Canterbury CI *IP* IP1 .... 31 J1
Canterbury Gdns *HADL* IP7 .... 29 F4
Capel CI *FX* IP11 .... 36 E6
Capel Dr *FX* IP11 .... 42 E5
Capel Hall La *FX* IP11 .... 37 F6
Carders CI *HADL* IP7 .... 29 F6
Cardew Drift *KESG* IP5 .... 20 D5
Cardiff Av *CHTY* IP2 .... 24 A6
Cardigan St *IP* IP1 .... 2 B1
Cardinalls Rd *SMKT* IP14 .... 4 E2

Cardinal St *IP* IP1 .... 2 D5
Carlford CI *KESG* IP5 .... 21 H6
Carlton Rd *KESG* IP5 .... 20 B6
Carlton Wk *HADL* IP7 .... 29 F6
Carlton Wy *IPNE* IP4 .... 18 D5
Carlyle CI *IP* IP1 .... 17 J1
Carmarthen CI *CHTY* IP2 .... 23 K6
Carmelites PI *WDBR* IP12 ...... 15 H4
Carol Av *WDBR* IP12 .... 21 H4
Carolbrook Rd *CHTY* IP2 .... 23 H5
Carol CI *FX* IP11 .... 43 H5
Carriage CI *FX* IP11 .... 42 B2
Carriers Ct *RCOLE* CO7 .... 45 H2
Carr Rd *FX* IP11 .... 53 F4
Carr St *IPNE* IP4 .... 3 F3
Case La *RIPS/CAP* IP9 .... 39 H5
Castle CI *FX* IP11 .... 43 J4
Castle Gdns *KESG* IP5 .... 20 E6
Castlegate St *HAR* CO12 * 52 A4
Castle La *HADL* IP7 .... 28 D3
Castle Ri *HADL* IP7 .... 28 C3
Castle Rd *HADL* IP7 .... 28 C3
Castle St *WDBR* IP12 .... 15 G4
Catesbray *RIPS/CAP* IP9 .... 38 D2
Catherine Rd *WDBR* IP12 ...... 15 F3
Cattawade St *MGTR* CO11 ..... 46 C6
Catts CI *RIPS/CAP* IP9 .... 48 B5
Cattsfield *RIPS/CAP* IP9 .... 48 B5
Cauldwell Av *IPNE* IP4 .... 18 E6
Cauldwell Hall Rd *IPNE* IP4 ... 19 F6
The Causeway *NHMKT* IP6 .... 6 E5
Cavan Rd *IP* IP1 .... 17 H4
Cavendish Gdns *FX* IP11 .... 36 E6
Cavendish Rd *FX* IP11 .... 36 D6
  FX IP11 .... 53 H1
  SMKT IP14 .... 4 C3
Cavendish St *IPSE* IP3 .... 3 K6
Cecilia St *IP* IP1 .... 2 D5
Cecil Rd *IP* IP1 .... 2 C2
Cedar Av *KESG* IP5 .... 26 B1
Cedar CI *MGTR* CO11 .... 46 D4
Cedarcroft Rd *IP* IP1 .... 17 J3
Cedars La *RIPS/CAP* IP9 .... 38 D2
Cedar Wk *NHMKT* IP6 .... 6 E4
Celestion Dr *IPSE* IP3 .... 25 F3
Cemetery La *IPNE* IP4 .... 18 D5
  RCOLE CO7 .... 45 F3
  WDBR IP12 .... 15 F5
Cemetery Rd *IPNE* IP4 .... 3 J2
Central Av *IPSE* IP3 .... 33 J1
Century Dr *KESG* IP5 .... 26 E1
Chaffinch Wy *SMKT* IP14 .... 5 G2
Chainhouse Rd *NHMKT* IP6 ...... 6 E5
Chalkeith Rd *NHMKT* IP6 .... 7 F6
Chalk Hill La *NHMKT* IP6 .... 10 B1
Chalkners CI *RIPS/CAP* IP9 .... 38 E2
Chalon St *IP* IP1 .... 2 C4
Chamberlain Wy *RIPW* IP8 ..... 23 F5
Chancery Rd *IP* IP1 .... 2 B5
Chandos CI *WDBR* IP12 .... 21 H3
Chandos Dr *WDBR* IP12 .... 21 H3
Chantry CI *FRAM/WMKT* IP13 ... 9 H3
Chantry Gn *CHTY* IP2 .... 23 G4
Chantry Pk *CHTY* IP2 * 23 G2
Chapel CI *RIPS/CAP* IP9 .... 38 E2
Chapel Fld *RIPW* IP8 .... 16 D3
Chapel La *FRAM/WMKT* IP13 .... 8 D4
  FRAM/WMKT IP13 .... 13 J4
  NHMKT IP6 .... 10 D3
  RIPW IP8 .... 22 D6
Chapel Rd *FRAM/WMKT* IP13 . 13 J4
Chapel St *WDBR* IP12 .... 15 H4
Chaplin Rd *RCOLE* CO7 .... 45 G2
Charles Av *FRAM/WMKT* IP13 . 13 H3
Charles Rd *FX* IP11 .... 53 F3
Charles St *IP* IP1 .... 2 D2
Charlotte's *RIPW* IP8 .... 22 C6
Charlton Av *IP* IP1 .... 17 J3
Chartwell CI *IPNE* IP4 .... 25 F2
The Chase *KESG* IP5 .... 21 H6
  MGTR CO11 .... 47 F4
Chatsworth Crs *CHTY* IP2 ...... 23 K5
  FX IP11 .... 42 B3
Chatsworth Dr *IPNE* IP4 .... 25 F2
Chattisham CI *SMKT* IP14 .... 5 F6
Chaucer Rd *FX* IP11 .... 53 H1
  IP IP1 .... 17 J2
Chelsea CI *IP* IP1 .... 17 J4
Chelsworth Av *IPNE* IP4 .... 18 C4
Chelsworth Rd *FX* IP11 .... 53 F1
Chelsworth Wy *SMKT* IP14 .... 5 F6
Cheltenham Av *IP* IP1 .... 18 A4
Chepstow Rd *FX* IP11 .... 42 E5
  IP IP1 .... 18 A1
Chequers Ri *NHMKT* IP6 .... 10 C1
Cherry Blossom CI *RIPW* IP8 .. 22 C6
Cherry Gardens La *IPNE* IP4 ... 19 G6
Cherry Tree Rd *SMKT* IP14 .... 4 D1

  WDBR IP12 .... 15 G5
Cherry Wd *RIPW* IP8 * 30 C2
Chesapeake Rd *IPSE* IP3 .... 33 F2
Chesham Rd *CHTY* IP2 .... 2 C7
Chessington Gdns *IP* IP1 .... 17 J5
Chesterfield Dr *IP* IP1 .... 17 J3
Chester Rd *FX* IP11 .... 42 E6
Chesterton CI *KESG* IP5 .... 23 J4
Chestnut CI *KESG* IP5 .... 19 K4
  SMKT IP14 .... 5 H1
Chestnut Dr *NHMKT* IP6 .... 11 F4
Chestnut Gv *SMKT* IP14 .... 5 F4
The Chestnuts *CHTY* IP2 .... 23 F5
Chevalier Rd *FX* IP11 .... 43 G6
Chevallier St *IP* IP1 .... 17 K6
Childer Rd *SMKT* IP14 .... 4 E3
Childers CI *RIPS/CAP* IP9 ...... 51 G4
Childers Fld *FX* IP11 .... 42 C5
Chilton Av *SMKT* IP14 .... 4 D3
Chilton Rd *IPSE* IP3 .... 25 H3
Chilton Wy *SMKT* IP14 .... 5 F4
Chisnall CI *HADL* IP7 .... 28 E3
Christchurch Ct *IPNE* IP4 * 3 G2
Christchurch Dr *WDBR* IP12 ... 14 E6
Christchurch St *IPNE* IP4 .... 3 G2
Church CI *KESG* IP5 .... 20 C5
  KIR/NAC IP10 .... 27 H6
  NHMKT IP6 .... 7 G1
  RCOLE CO7 * 38 A2
Church Crs *RIPW* IP8 .... 22 D7
Church Gn *RIPW* IP8 .... 16 E4
Church HI *RIPS/CAP* IP9 .... 49 F1
Churchill Av *HADL* IP7 .... 28 E3
  IPNE IP4 .... 25 F1
Churchill CI *WDBR* IP12 .... 21 J4
Churchill Crs *FRAM/WMKT* IP13 . 8 D2
Church La *FX* IP11 .... 42 A1
  KIR/NAC IP10 .... 37 F2
  KIR/NAC IP10 .... 35 F6
  KIR/NAC IP10 .... 27 H6
  MGTR CO11 .... 46 D4
  NHMKT IP6 .... 20 C1
  NHMKT IP6 .... 7 F2
  NHMKT IP6 .... 11 F3
  RIPS/CAP IP9 .... 50 C3
  RIPS/CAP IP9 .... 49 K4
  RIPW IP8 .... 30 A5
Churchman CI *WDBR* IP12 ..... 15 J1
Church Rd *FRAM/WMKT* IP13 . 14 C2
  FX IP11 .... 43 H4
  KIR/NAC IP10 .... 34 C1
  RIPS/CAP IP9 .... 48 C3
  RIPS/CAP IP9 .... 39 J1
  SMKT IP14 .... 4 E6
Church St *HADL* IP7 .... 28 E4
  RIPS/CAP IP9 .... 40 C4
  WDBR IP12 .... 15 H4
Church Ter *FRAM/WMKT* IP13 .. 8 D3
Church View CI *WDBR* IP12 ... 15 K2
Church Wk *RIPS/CAP* IP9 .... 41 H6
  SMKT IP14 .... 4 E3
Cinnabar CI *RIPW* IP8 .... 31 H1
Civic Dr *IP* IP1 .... 2 C2
Clapgate La *IPSE* IP3 .... 25 H5
Clare Av *WDBR* IP12 .... 15 F5
Clare CI *SMKT* IP14 .... 5 F4
Clarence Rd *IPSE* IP3 .... 25 G4
Clare Rd *IPNE* IP4 .... 18 E5
Clarkson St *IP* IP1 .... 2 A2
Claude St *IP* IP1 .... 2 D7
Claverton Wy *IPNE* IP4 .... 25 K2
  IPSE IP3 .... 25 K4
Clayton Ct *WDBR* IP12 .... 14 E4
Clearwing CI *RIPW* IP8 .... 31 H1
Clementine Gdns *IPNE* IP4 .... 25 F3
Clench CI *IPNE* IP4 .... 3 G6
Cliff La *IPSE* IP3 .... 24 D4
Clifford Rd *IPNE* IP4 .... 3 K6
Cliff Rd *FX* IP11 .... 43 J3
  IPSE IP3 .... 24 D6
Clifton Wy *CHTY* IP2 .... 23 G3
Clifton Wd *RIPS/CAP* IP9 ...... 49 F1
Clive Av *IP* IP1 .... 18 A3
Cloncurry Gdns *FX* IP11 .... 53 F7
Clopton Gdns *HADL* IP7 .... 28 E3
Clopton Rd *NHMKT* IP6 .... 12 B6
Clovelly CI *IPNE* IP4 .... 26 A3
Clover CI *CHTY* IP2 .... 23 J1
  IPNE IP4 .... 6 E5
Clump Fld *CHTY* IP2 * 23 J3
Coachmans Ct *IP* IP1 * 2 E1
Coachman's Paddock
  RIPS/CAP IP9 .... 49 F2
Cobbold Ms *IPNE* IP4 .... 3 G4
Cobbold Rd *FX* IP11 .... 43 F4
  WDBR IP12 .... 15 G3
Cobbold St *IPNE* IP4 .... 3 F4
Cobden PI *IPNE* IP4 .... 3 G3
Cobham Rd *IPSE* IP3 .... 25 H4

Coddenham Rd NHMKT IP6........7 F5
Cody Rd IPSE IP3.........25 H6
Colchester Rd IPNE IP4........18 E4
Cold Store Rd FX IP11.........52 E3
Cole Ness Rd IPSE IP3.........33 F1
Coleridge Rd IP IP1.........17 J2
College Gn FX IP11.........43 H6
College St IPNE IP4.........2 E5
Collett's Wk WDBR IP12.........15 F4
Collimer Cl RIPS/CAP IP9.........40 C3
Collingwood Av IPSE IP3.........25 G5
Collingwood Flds RCOLE CO7......45 F1
Collingwood Rd WDBR IP12......15 G3
Collinson's CHTY IP2.........23 F2
Colneis Rd IP IP11.........43 F4
Coltsfoot Rd CHTY IP2.........23 H3
Columbia Cl KESG IP5.........20 B6
Columbine Gdns CHTY IP2.......23 H2
Combs La SMKT IP14.........4 A4
Combs Wood Dr SMKT IP14......4 E6
Commercial Rd IP IP1.........2 C6
Common Quay IPNE IP4 *.........3 F5
Conach Rd WDBR IP12.........15 F4
Congreve Rd IP IP1.........17 K2
Coniston Cl FX IP11.........43 K3
Coniston Rd IPSE IP3.........25 G5
Connaught Rd IP IP1.........17 C3
Constable Rd FX IP11.........43 G6
    IPNE IP4.........18 C6
Constantine Rd IP IP1.........2 B5
Constitution Hl IP IP1.........18 A5
    NHMKT IP6.........
Convalescent Hl FX IP11.........53 J1
Conway St IP CHTY IP2.........24 A5
    FX IP11.........43 H3
Cooks Cl KESG IP5.........21 F5
Coombers RIPS/CAP IP9.........38 D2
Coopers Rd KESG IP5.........21 J6
Coopers Wy NHMKT IP6.........10 E2
Copleston Rd IPNE IP4.........25 G2
Copperfield Rd CHTY IP2.........23 H2
Coppice Cl WDBR IP12.........15 H3
Coprolite St IPSE IP3.........3 H5
Copse Cl KESG IP5.........21 G6
Copswood Cl KESG IP5.........21 G6
Coral Dr IP IP1.........17 C4
Coram St HADL IP7.........28 B4
Corder Rd IPNE IP4.........18 C5
Cordwinders RCOLE CO7.........45 J4
Cordy's La HADL IP7.........28 D4
Corks La SMKT IP14.........4 D4
Cormorant Dr SMKT IP14.........5 C4
Cornflower Cl CHTY IP2.........23 H3
Cornhill IP IP1.........2 D3
Cornwall Rd FX IP11.........42 D5
Coronation Dr FX IP11.........53 F1
Coronation Rd IPNE IP4.........25 G2
Corporation Av CHTY IP2.........31 K1
Corton Rd IPSE IP3.........25 G6
Cosford Rd HADL IP7.........28 E1
Cotman Rd IPSE IP3.........25 F6
Cotswold Av IP IP1.........18 A4
Cottesford Cl HADL IP7.........28 C4
Cottingham Rd RIPW IP8.........22 E6
The Courts RIPS IP3.........43 G6
Cowell St CHTY IP2.........24 B4
Cowley Rd FX IP11.........42 A4
Cowper St IPNE IP4.........25 G1
Cowslip Cl CHTY IP2.........23 H3
Cowslip Wy NHMKT IP6.........6 E3
Cox Cl KESG IP5.........26 C1
Cox La IP IP1.........3 F4
Coytes Gdns IP IP1.........2 D4
Crabbe St IPNE IP4.........25 F1
Craig Cl FX IP11.........36 E6
Cranberry Sq IPSE IP3.........33 H2
Cranborne Cha IPNE IP4.........19 F4
Crane Cl WDBR IP12.........14 E6
Cranwell Crs IPSE IP3.........25 H6
Cranwell Gv KESG IP5.........21 H5
Cranworth Cl FRAM/WMKT IP13...13 H4
Cranworth Rd HADL IP7.........29 F6
Crawford La KESG IP5.........20 D6
Creeting Rd SMKT IP14.........5 F3
Crepping Hall Dr RIPS/CAP IP9...48 B3
Crescent Rd FX IP11.........43 F6
    IP IP1.........2 B2
The Crescent FRAM/WMKT IP13...8 C3
    SMKT IP14.........5 F5
Cricket Hill Rd FX IP11.........42 C5
Crockatt Hl HADL IP7.........29 F4
Crocus Cl CHTY IP2.........23 H3
Crofton Rd IPNE IP4.........24 B4
Croft St CHTY IP2.........23 H3
Cromarty Rd IPNE IP4.........19 C5
Cromer Rd IP IP1.........17 J5
Crompton Rd CHTY IP2.........17 H6

Cromwell Sq IP IP1.........2 D4
Crossgate Fld FX IP11.........42 D5
Crossley Gdns IP IP1.........17 F3
Cross St FX IP11.........42 D4
Crotchets Cl RIPS/CAP IP9.......38 E2
Croutel Rd FX IP11.........43 G5
Crowe Hall La RIPS/CAP IP9.....48 C5
Crowe St SMKT IP14.........4 E3
Crowland Cl CHTY IP2.........23 K5
Crow La SMKT IP14.........4 E4
Crowley Rd NHMKT IP6.........6 E4
Crown & Anchor Ms IP IP1 *......2 D3
Crown Cl WDBR IP12.........21 J3
Crown La FRAM/WMKT IP13.......8 D3
Crown Paddock NHMKT IP6 *.....6 E4
Crown Pl WDBR IP12.........15 H5
Crown St FX IP11.........42 D5
    IP IP1.........2 C3
    NHMKT IP6.........6 E4
    SMKT IP14.........4 E2
Crowswell Ct FX IP11.........36 E6
Croxton Cl KIR/NAC IP10.........37 F3
Crozier Ms IPNE IP4.........25 G1
Cuckfield Av IPSE IP3.........25 K4
Culford Wk FX IP11.........52 E1
Cullingham Rd IP IP1.........23 K1
Cumberland Cl IP IP1.........43 J4
Cumberland Ms WDBR IP12.....15 H5
Cumberland St IP IP1.........2 B1
    WDBR IP12.........15 G5
Curlew Rd CHTY IP2.........23 C4
Curriers' La IP IP1.........2 C4
Curtis Cl RIPW IP8.........23 F6
Curtis Wy KESG IP5.........20 E6
Curwen Rd SMKT IP14.........4 D2
Cutlers La RCOLE CO7.........45 J1
Cutler St IP IP1.........2 D5

D

Daffodil Cl CHTY IP2.........23 H4
Daimler Rd IP IP1.........17 F3
Dains Pl FX IP11.........42 B3
Daires La WDBR IP12.........15 K2
Dale Hall La IP IP1.........18 A3
Dales Rd IP IP1.........17 K4
Dales Vw RIPW IP8.........30 B1
Dales View Rd IP IP1.........17 K4
Dallingham Rd FRAM/WMKT IP13...8 A4
Dalton Rd IP IP1.........17 H6
Damselfly Rd IPSE IP3.........33 H1
Dandalan Cl IP IP1.........17 H6
Danes Cl SMKT IP14.........4 D4
Danescourt Av SMKT IP14.........4 D4
Darrell Rd FX IP11.........53 F3
Darsham Cl FX IP11.........42 D5
Darter Cl IPSE IP3.........33 H1
Darwin Rd IPNE IP4.........24 E2
Dashwood Cl RIPW IP8.........23 G6
Daundy Cl CHTY IP2.........23 C2
Davey Cl IPSE IP3.........24 E6
Dawes Cl RIPS/CAP IP9.........38 D2
Dawson Drift KESG IP5.........20 D6
Dawson Dr FX IP11.........42 B2
Days Gn RIPS/CAP IP9.........38 D2
Days Rd RIPS/CAP IP9.........38 D3
Dazeley's La RCOLE CO7.........45 K5
Deacon Cl FX IP11.........43 J4
Deben Av KESG IP5.........21 C5
Deben Rd IP IP1.........17 J4
    WDBR IP12.........15 J4
The Debenside WDBR IP12 *.....15 K2
Deben Valley Dr KESG IP5.......20 D6
Deben Wy FX IP11.........53 G1
De Brink-on-the-Green
    KESG IP5 *.........21 H6
Dedham Mi RCOLE CO7 *.........44 D6
Dedham Pl IPNE IP4 *.........3 F4
Dedham Rd RCOLE CO7.........44 D4
Defoe Rd IP IP1.........17 K1
Delf Cl HADL IP7.........29 F4
Delius Rd SMKT IP14.........4 D2
Dellwood Av FX IP11.........43 H5
Demesne Gdns KESG IP5.........21 H5
Demoiselle Crs IPSE IP3.........33 H1
Denmark Gdns RIPS/CAP IP9....49 F1
Denton Cl CHTY IP2.........23 C5
Derby Cl IPNE IP4.........25 F2
Derby Rd IPSE IP3.........25 F3
Dereham Av IPSE IP3.........24 E4
Derwent Rd IPSE IP3.........24 E4
Devlin Rd IPSE IP3.........22 E6
Devon Rd FX IP11.........42 E5
    SMKT IP14.........5 H1
Devonshire Rd IPSE IP3.........24 A5
Dewar La KESG IP5.........20 D6
Dhobi Pl IP IP1.........17 J6

Dial La IP IP1.........2 E3
Diamond Cl IP IP1.........17 F4
Dickens Rd CHTY IP2.........23 H1
Dickinson Ter KESG IP5.........20 E6
Didsbury Cl CHTY IP2.........23 C5
Digby Cl KESG IP5.........27 H1
Digby Rd IPNE IP4.........19 H6
Dillwyn St IP IP1.........2 A3
Dillwyn St West IP IP1.........2 A3
Ditchingham Gv KESG IP5.......25 K1
Ditton Wy IPSE IP3.........25 C6
Dobbs Drift KESG IP5.........21 G6
Dobbs La KIR/NAC IP10.........27 F2
Dock Basin FX IP11 *.........52 E4
Dock La WDBR IP12.........15 K2
Dock St CHTY IP2.........53 F4
The Docks FX IP11.........52 E4
Dock St CHTY IP2.........2 E6
Doctor Watson's La KESG IP5...20 B4
Dodmans RIPS/CAP IP9.........38 E2
Dodson V KESG IP5.........20 D6
Dogs Head St IP IP1.........2 E4
Dogwood Cl IPSE IP3.........25 J5
Dombey Rd CHTY IP2.........23 H2
Donegal Rd IP IP1.........17 C3
Donkey La RCOLE CO7.........44 D4
Dooley Rd FX IP11.........52 E1
Dorchester Rd IPSE IP3.........25 G4
Doric Pl WDBR IP12.........15 H4
Dorset Cl IPNE IP4.........18 E4
Dotterel Wy SMKT IP14.........5 C3
Dovedale Cl FX IP11.........53 F1
Dove Gdns SMKT IP14.........5 H5
Dover Rd IPSE IP3.........25 G3
Dove St IPNE IP4.........3 H3
Downham Bvd IPSE IP3.........33 H1
Downing Cl CHTY IP2.........23 J5
    WDBR IP12.........15 F3
Downside SMKT IP14.........4 C3
Downside Cl CHTY IP2.........31 J1
The Downs FX IP11.........42 C5
Drake Av IPSE IP3.........25 G5
Drake Cl SMKT IP14.........4 B3
Drake Sq North IPSE IP3.........25 G5
Drake Sq South IPSE IP3.........25 G4
Drapers Cl HADL IP7.........29 F4
Draymans Wy IPSE IP3.........24 D4
Drift Cots FX IP11 *.........43 H4
The Driftway
    FRAM/WMKT IP13.........13 J4
    IP IP1.........25 C1
The Drive KESG IP5.........21 K5
Drover's Ct FX IP11.........42 A2
Drum Fld RCOLE CO7.........44 B4
Drury Rd NHMKT IP6.........11 F3
Drybridge Hl WDBR IP12.......15 F5
Dryden Rd IP IP1.........17 K2
Duckamere RIPW IP8.........16 D4
Dukes Cl FX IP11.........43 J4
Duke's Meadow WDBR IP12.....14 E6
Duke St HADL IP7.........28 E5
    IPSE IP3.........3 H6
Dumbarton Rd IPNE IP4.........19 C5
Dunlin Rd CHTY IP2.........23 H5
Dunlop Rd CHTY IP2.........23 J1
Dunn Cl HADL IP7.........29 F5
Dunnoch Cl SMKT IP14.........5 H4
Dunton Gv HADL IP7.........28 E6
Durrant Rd HADL IP7.........28 E3
Dyer Ct HADL IP7.........29 C5
Dyke Rd FX IP11.........52 D2
Dykes St IP IP1.........2 D1

E

Eagles Cl FX IP11.........42 E6
Eagle St IPNE IP4.........3 F4
Eagle Wy KESG IP5.........21 H5
Earls Cl FX IP11.........43 J4
Eastcliff FX IP11.........43 K3
East End La RCOLE CO7.........46 C3
East End Rd RCOLE CO7.........46 A3
Eastern Cl IPNE IP4.........26 A3
Eastland Ct FX IP11.........42 C3
East Lawn IPNE IP4.........19 H5
East Mill Gn RIPS/CAP IP9.......39 J5
Easton Rd FRAM/WMKT IP13......8 C1
East Rw RIPS/CAP IP9 *.........49 F1
Eastward Pl SMKT IP14.........4 D2

Eaton Cl FX IP11.........42 B3
Eaton Gdns FX IP11.........53 G2
Eccles Rd CHTY IP2.........23 C5
Eddowes Rd NHMKT IP6.........11 F2
Eden Rd IPNE IP4.........25 G2
Edgar Av SMKT IP14.........4 E6
Edgecomb Rd SMKT IP14.........4 E6
Edgeworth Rd CHTY IP2.........23 H5
Edinburgh Cl SMKT IP14.........5 F2
Edinburgh Gdns NHMKT IP6......11 F2
Edmonton Cl KESG IP5.........20 B6
Edmonton Rd KESG IP5.........20 B5
Edward Cl IP IP1.........17 J5
Edwin Av WDBR IP12.........15 G2
Edwin Panks Rd HADL IP7.......29 F4
Egglestone Cl CHTY IP2.........23 J6
Eldred Cl IP IP1.........17 G5
Eliot Wy SMKT IP14.........4 C1
Elizabeth Wy FX IP11.........53 F1
    SMKT IP14.........5 F3
Ellenbrook Rd CHTY IP2.........23 G6
    RIPW IP8.........31 H1
Elliott St IP IP1.........2 A2
Elm Cl MGTR CO11.........46 D4
Elmcroft La FX IP11.........43 H3
Elmcroft Rd FX IP11.........17 K3
Elmers La KESG IP5.........20 E6
Elm Gdns FX IP11.........42 B3
Elmham Dr KIR/NAC IP10.........34 C1
Elmhurst Ct WDBR IP12 *.......15 J4
Elmhurst Dr IPSE IP3.........24 E4
Elm La RIPS/CAP IP9.........38 E2
    RIPW IP8.........30 B1
Elm Rd FRAM/WMKT IP13.........8 C3
    KESG IP5.........20 A6
    RCOLE CO7.........45 F2
    SMKT IP14.........4 D3
Elmsett Cl SMKT IP14.........5 G6
Elm St IP IP1.........2 D3
Elsmere Rd IP IP1.........18 B5
Elton Pk CHTY IP2.........23 C1
Ely Rd IPNE IP4.........18 E4
    NHMKT IP6.........11 G2
Emerald Cl KESG IP5.........20 D5
Emlen St IP IP1.........2 A3
Emmanuel Cl CHTY IP2.........23 J5
Emmerson Wy HADL IP7.........28 E3
Ennerdale Cl FX IP11.........43 J3
Epsom Dr IP IP1.........18 A1
Ernleigh Rd IPNE IP4.........25 C1
Erwarton Wk RIPS/CAP IP9......50 C2
Essex Wy IPSE IP3.........25 K6
    RCOLE CO7.........44 B6
Estuary Crs RIPS/CAP IP9.......51 H5
Estuary Dr FX IP11.........43 J3
Estuary Rd RIPS/CAP IP9.......51 G5
Europa Wy IP IP1.........17 G5
Eustace Rd IP IP1.........17 H5
Euston Av IPNE IP4.........26 A1
Euston Ct FX IP11.........42 B6
Evabrook Cl CHTY IP2.........23 H6
Everton Crs IP IP1.........17 J4
Evesham Cl CHTY IP2.........23 K5
Exeter Rd FX IP11.........42 E5
    IPSE IP3.........25 G3
    NHMKT IP6.........11 G2
Exmoor Rd FX IP11.........42 E4

F

Factory La MGTR CO11.........46 C6
Fairbairn Av KESG IP5.........20 E6
Fairfax Gdns NHMKT IP6.........7 F5
Fairfield Av FX IP11.........43 F5
Fairfield Hl SMKT IP14.........4 E3
Fairfield Rd IPSE IP3.........25 F5
The Fairways IPNE IP4.........25 K2
Falcon St FX IP11.........42 D4
    IP IP1.........2 D4
Falkenham Rd KIR/NAC IP10.....17 J1
Falmouth Cl KESG IP5.........26 C1
Faraday Rd IPSE IP3.........24 E2
Farina Cl IP IP1.........17 J6
Farlingayes WDBR IP12.........15 F2
Farriers Cl KESG IP5.........21 H5
Farrier's Rd SMKT IP14.........4 D6
Farriers Went FX IP11.........42 C3
Farthing Rd IP IP1.........17 F6
Farthings Went RIPS/CAP IP9...39 F1
Faulkeners Wy FX IP11.........42 B2
Fawley Cl IPNE IP4.........19 H6
Fayrefield Rd WDBR IP12.......15 J2
Featherbroom Gdns
    FRAM/WMKT IP13.........8 D4
Feathers Fld FX IP11.........42 C5
Felaw St CHTY IP2.........3 F7
Felix Cl KESG IP5.........20 C6

Felix Rd *FX* IP11............43 G6
IPSE IP3...............25 H5
SMKT IP14................5 H1
Felixstowe Rd *IPSE* IP3......25 F3
KIR/NAC IP10............34 B1
WDBR IP12..............21 J4
Fellbrigg Av *KESG* IP5.......26 A1
Felsham Ct *SMKT* IP14.........5 C6
Fen Br *RCOLE* CO7...........45 F5
Fenbridge La *RCOLE* CO7......45 F5
Fen Bright Cir *RIPW* IP8......33 H2
Fen Meadow *FX* IP11..........42 B2
Fenn Cl *SMKT* IP14............4 E6
Fentons Wy *KESG* IP5.........20 D6
Fen Vw *RIPW* IP8.............30 B3
Ferguson Wy *KESG* IP5........20 C6
Ferndown Rd *FX* IP11.........43 G5
Fernhayes Cl *CHTY* IP2.......25 H3
Fernhill Cl *WDBR* IP12........15 H3
Ferry La *FX* IP11............52 E1
Ferry Rd *FX* IP11............43 H1
Fiddlers La *RCOLE* CO7.......45 G2
Fieldfare Cl *SMKT* IP14.......5 G3
Field Vw *KIR/NAC* IP10.......35 H1
Fife Rd *IPNE* IP4.............19 G4
Finbars Wk *IPNE* IP4...........3 K4
Finborough Cl *KESG* IP5......26 A1
Finborough Rd *SMKT* IP14......4 C3
Finch Cl *SMKT* IP14...........5 J4
Finchley Rd *IPNE* IP4.........3 H2
Findley Cl *RIPS/CAP* IP9.....48 B5
Finney's Drift *KIR/NAC* IP10..34 D4
Fir Cl *FRAM/WMKT* IP13........8 D2
Fircroft Rd *IP* IP1..........18 A2
Firebronds Rd *RIPS/CAP* IP9..49 F2
Firecrest Dr *SMKT* IP14.......5 G2
Firefly Wy *IPSE* IP3.........25 C6
Firmin Cl *IP* IP1.............2 A3
Fir Tree Hl *RIPS/CAP* IP9....49 H3
Fir Tree La *NHMKT* IP6.......11 F3
Fir Tree Ri *RIPW* IP8........23 F5
Fishbane Cl *IPSE* IP3........33 F1
Fisher's La *RCOLE* CO7.......46 C2
The Fishers *IPSE* IP3........20 D6
Fishponds La *RIPS/CAP* IP9...49 G2
Fitzgerald Rd *RIPW* IP8......16 D4
WDBR IP12..............15 H3
Fitzmaurice Rd *IPSE* IP3.....25 G4
Fitzroy St *IP* IP1............2 E2
Fitzwilliam Cl *CHTY* IP2.....23 J5
WDBR IP12..............15 F5
Five Acres *RIPS/CAP* IP9.....49 F2
Flatford Cl *SMKT* IP14.........5 F6
Flatford Rd *RCOLE* CO7.......45 G4
Fleetwood Av *FX* IP11........43 F5
Fleetwood Cl *NHMKT* IP6.......7 C1
Fleetwood Rd *FX* IP11........43 G5
Fletcher Cl *NHMKT* IP6.......10 E2
Fletcher Rd *IPSE* IP3........33 F1
Fletchers La *KESG* IP5.......20 E5
Flindell Dr *RIPW* IP8........16 D3
Flint Cl *CHTY* IP2...........24 A5
Fiordon Rd *NHMKT* IP6..........7 F3
Florence Vls *MGTR* CO11 *....46 D4
Foden Av *IP* IP1.............17 F3
Folly La *RIPW* IP8...........30 A5
Fonnereau Rd *IP* IP1...........2 D1
Ford Cl *SMKT* IP14............5 F5
Fordham Pl *IPNE* IP4.........26 A2
Ford View Rd *SMKT* IP14.......5 F5
Fore Hamlet *IPSE* IP3.........3 H5
Forester Cl *RIPW* IP8........31 G1
Foresters Wk *NHMKT* IP6......10 E2
Forest La *KESG* IP5..........27 H1
Fore St *IPNE* IP4.............3 G5
Forfar Cl *FX* IP11...........19 G4
Forge Cl *KIR/NAC* IP10.......27 H6
Foundation St *IPNE* IP4.......3 F5
Foundry La *IP* IP1............2 E5
Fountains Rd *CHTY* IP2.......23 H6
Foxglove Av *NHMKT* IP6........6 E6
Foxglove Crs *IPSE* IP3.......25 K6
Foxgrove Gdns *FX* IP11.......43 H5
Foxgrove La *FX* IP11.........43 H5
Foxhall Cl *RCOLE* CO7 *......45 G1
Foxhall Flds *RCOLE* CO7......45 F2
Foxhall Rd *IPSE* IP3..........3 K5
KIR/NAC IP10...........26 E2
Fox Lea *KESG* IP5............21 F5
Foxley Cl *IPSE* IP3..........25 J3
Foxtail Rd *IPSE* IP3.........33 J1
Foxwood Crs *IPNE* IP4........26 A2
Frampton Rd *IPSE* IP3........33 F1
Franciscan Wy *IP* IP1.........2 D4
Francis Cl *KESG* IP5.........21 F5
Franklin Rd *IPSE* IP3........25 G5
Fraser Rd *IP* IP1............17 J6
RIPW IP8..............16 E2
Freehold Rd *IPNE* IP4........25 F1

NHMKT IP6..................6 D3
Freeman Cl *HADL* IP7.........28 E3
Freston Hi *RIPS/CAP* IP9.....32 D5
Freston Rd *IPSE* IP3.........33 H1
Freston St *RIPS/CAP* IP9.....32 C6
Friars Bridge Rd *IP* IP1......2 C4
Friars Cl *FX* IP11...........43 J4
Friars Ct *WDBR* IP12.........15 K2
Friars Rd *HADL* IP7..........28 D5
Friars St *IP* IP1.............2 D4
Friends Wk *KESG* IP5.........20 E5
Fritton Cl *CHTY* IP2.........23 K6
Frobisher Rd *IPSE* IP3.......24 E6
Frog Hall La *HADL* IP7.......29 F4
Frogs Aly *RIPS/CAP* IP9......41 K6
Front Rd *IPSE* IP3...........33 J1
Fuchsia La *IPSE* IP3.........25 F2
Fullers Cl *HADL* IP7.........29 F4
Fullers Rd *NHMKT* IP6 *......18 D1
Fuller's Fld *NHMKT* IP6......18 D1
Furness Cl *CHTY* IP2.........31 J1
Fynn Rd *WDBR* IP12...........14 E6
Fynn Valley Wk *KESG* IP5.....20 A1

G

Gaell Crs *HADL* IP7..........29 F5
Gainsborough La *IPSE* IP3....32 E1
Gainsborough Rd *FX* IP11.....43 F6
IPNE IP4..............18 C5
SMKT IP14...............4 C5
Gallows Hi *HADL* IP7.........28 D3
Galway Av *IP* IP1............17 H4
Gandish Cl *RCOLE* CO7 *......45 H4
Gandish Rd *RCOLE* CO7.......45 J3
Ganges Rd *RIPS/CAP* IP9.....51 G5
Gannet Rd *CHTY* IP2..........23 H4
Ganymede Cl *IP* IP1..........17 G6
Garden Cl *RIPS/CAP* IP9......50 E2
Garden Fld *FX* IP11..........42 D5
Garfield Cl *FX* IP11.........53 H1
Garfield Rd *FX* IP11.........53 H1
Garrick Wy *IP* IP1...........17 K2
Garrison La *FX* IP11.........53 H1
Garrods *RIPS/CAP* IP9........39 F2
The Garrods *KESG* IP5........26 C1
Gaston End *RCOLE* CO7........45 C2
Gaston St *RCOLE* CO7.........45 C3
Gatacre Rd *IP* IP1...........17 K6
Gate Farm Rd *RIPS/CAP* IP9...51 H4
Gaye St *IP* IP1...............2 B2
Gayfer Av *KESG* IP5..........21 G5
Gaymers La *FX* IP11..........42 A2
Generals Ms *FX* IP11.........42 C5
Geneva Av *KESG* IP5..........21 K5
Geneva Rd *IP* IP1.............2 C2
George Frost Cl *IPNE* IP4....18 C6
George St *HADL* IP7..........29 F4
Geralds Av *IPNE* IP4.........25 F2
Gibbons St *IP* IP1............2 A3
Gibson Cl *IPSE* IP3..........25 H5
Gifford Cl *RIPS/CAP* IP9.....49 F1
Giffords Pl *IPSE* IP3........26 A1
Gilbert Cl *NHMKT* IP6.........6 D4
Giles Ct *NHMKT* IP6 *........11 F2
Gippeswyk Av *CHTY* IP2........2 A7
Gippeswyk Rd *CHTY* IP2........2 B7
Gipping Pl *SMKT* IP14.........4 E2
Gipping Rd *NHMKT* IP6........10 D2
Gippingstone Rd *RIPW* IP8....16 D2
Gipping Valley River Pth *IP* IP1..2 C6
RIPW IP8..............16 D2
SMKT IP14..............5 G5
Gipping Wy *RIPW* IP8.........22 E1
SMKT IP14.............5 F3
Gipsy La *NHMKT* IP6..........6 D3
Girton Cl *WDBR* IP12.........14 E5
Girton Wy *CHTY* IP2..........23 H6
Gladstone Rd *IPSE* IP3........3 K5
WDBR IP12.............15 H4
Glamorgan Rd *CHTY* IP2.......24 A4
Glanville Pl *KESG* IP5.......26 C1
Glanville Rd *HADL* IP7.......29 F6
Glastonbury Cl *CHTY* IP2.....23 J6
Glebe Cl *RIPW* IP8...........22 E1
Glebe End *RIPS/CAP* IP9......39 F5
Glebe Wy *NHMKT* IP6..........11 F1
Glemham Dr *IPNE* IP4.........26 A3
Glemsford Cl *FX* IP11........53 F1
Glemsford Rd *SMKT* IP14.......5 F5
Glenavon Rd *IP* IP1..........19 J6
Glencoe Rd *IPNE* IP4.........19 H4
Gleneagles Cl *FX* IP11.......43 H4
Gleneagles Dr *IPNE* IP4......25 J2
Glenfield Av *FX* IP11........43 F4
Glenhurst Av *IPNE* IP4.......19 G5

Glevering Br *FRAM/WMKT* IP13..8 C1
Gloster Rd *KESG* IP5.........21 J6
Gloucester Rd *KESG* IP5......25 F5
Godbold Cl *KESG* IP5.........20 E6
Goddard Rd *IP* IP1...........17 F2
Goddard Rd East *IP* IP1......17 G2
Godfrey's Wd *WDBR* IP12......15 H3
Golden Lion La *HAR* CO12.....52 A5
Goldcrest Rd *CHTY* IP2.......23 G4
Goldsmith Rd *IP* IP1.........17 H1
Golf Rd *FX* IP11.............43 J5
Gonville Cl *WDBR* IP12.......15 F4
Goodman Gv *KESG* IP5.........21 F6
Goodwood Cl *IP* IP1..........18 A1
Goosander Rd *SMKT* IP14.......5 G3
Gordon Rd *IPNE* IP4..........19 F6
Goring Rd *IPNE* IP4..........25 G1
Gorsehayes *CHTY* IP2.........24 A4
Gorse Rd *IPSE* IP3...........25 G5
Gosford Wy *FX* IP11..........43 H4
Gostling Pl *KESG* IP5........21 F5
Gowers Cl *KESG* IP5..........21 F6
Gower St *CHTY* IP2............2 E6
Gowle Rd *SMKT* IP14...........4 D1
Goyfield Av *FX* IP11.........42 E6
Grafton Wy *IP* IP1............2 D5
Graham Av *IP* IP1............18 A5
Graham Rd *FX* IP11...........42 E5
IP IP1................18 A6
Grange Cl *FX* IP11...........42 D5
KESG IP5..............21 F5
Grange Ct *WDBR* IP12.........15 J3
Grange Farm Av *FX* IP11......42 C6
Grange La *KESG* IP5..........21 F5
Grange Rd *FX* IP11...........42 C6
IPNE IP4...............3 J4
Grantchester Pl *KESG* IP5....20 B6
Grantham Crs *CHTY* IP2........2 A7
Granville Rd *FX* IP11........53 H1
Granville St *IP* IP1..........2 B2
Grasmere Av *FX* IP11.........43 J4
Grasmere Cl *IPSE* IP3........33 G1
Gravel Pit La *MGTR* CO11.....46 E3
Gray's Orch *KIR/NAC* IP10....37 F3
Great Colman St *IPNE* IP4.....2 E3
Great Eastern Sq *FX* IP11....43 F5
Great Fld *FX* IP11...........42 B2
Great Gipping St *IP* IP1......2 C4
Great Harlings *RIPS/CAP* IP9..51 G4
Great Tufts *RIPS/CAP* IP9....39 F2
Great Whip St *CHTY* IP2.......2 E6
Grebe Cl *CHTY* IP2...........23 H5
SMKT IP14..............4 B3
Green Crs *KIR/NAC* IP10......35 H1
Greenfinch Av *CHTY* IP2......23 G4
Green La *FRAM/WMKT* IP13......8 E4
NHMKT IP6.............19 H1
RCOLE CO7.............44 A2
WDBR IP12.............21 J3
Green Man Wy *WDBR* IP12......15 J3
Green Oak Gld *RIPW* IP8......31 G1
Greenspire Gv *RIPW* IP8......22 E5
The Greens *IPNE* IP4.........26 A4
The Green *FRAM/WMKT* IP13....13 H3
HADL IP7..............29 F4
Greenways *IP* IP1............18 A5
Greenwich Cl *IPSE* IP3.......24 D5
Greenwich Rd *IPSE* IP3.......24 D5
Greyfriars *IP* IP1............2 C4
Grey Friars Rd *IP* IP1........2 C4
Griffin Cl *CHTY* IP2 *.......24 C4
Grimwade Cl *MGTR* CO11.......46 D6
Grimwade St *IPNE* IP4.........3 G5
The Grindle *RIPW* IP8........16 C6
Grinstead Gdns *NHMKT* IP6.....7 F6
Grinstead Hi *NHMKT* IP6.......7 F6
Grosvenor Cl *IPNE* IP4.......18 D5
Grove Gdns *WDBR* IP12........15 F4
Grove Hi *RIPW* IP8...........31 F2
Grove La *IPNE* IP4............3 J4
RIPS/CAP IP9..........40 C6
Grove Ms *FX* IP11............42 E5
Grove Rd *FRAM/WMKT* IP13......8 A4
FX IP11...............43 F4
MGTR CO11.............46 D6
RIPS/CAP IP9..........39 J5
WDBR IP12.............14 E5
The Grove *IP* IP1............18 B3
KESG IP5..............21 H5
WDBR IP12.............15 J4
Grundisburgh Rd
FRAM/WMKT IP13.........13 H6
WDBR IP12.............15 F4
Guillemot Cl *SMKT* IP14.......5 G3
Gull La *FRAM/WMKT* IP13......13 G3
Gulpher Cots *FX* IP11 *......43 F2
Gulpher Rd *FX* IP11..........42 D1
Gurdon Rd *FRAM/WMKT* IP13....13 J3

Guston Gdns *KIR/NAC* IP10....37 F2
Guthrum Rd *HADL* IP7.........28 E4
Gwendoline Rd *IPNE* IP4......25 K3
Gymnasium St *IP* IP1..........2 B2

H

Hackney Ter *WDBR* IP12.......15 J3
Hadleigh Rd *CHTY* IP2........23 H1
RCOLE CO7.............45 F3
RIPW IP8..............23 F3
Hale Cl *CHTY* IP2............23 G5
Halesowen Cl *CHTY* IP2.......31 J1
Half Moon La *FRAM/WMKT* IP13..13 J3
Halford Ct *RIPW* IP8.........23 F1
Halifax Rd *CHTY* IP2.........24 A3
Hall Farm Cl *WDBR* IP12......15 J1
Hall Farm Rd *WDBR* IP12......15 K1
Hall Fld *FX* IP11............42 C5
Halliwell Rd *IPNE* IP4.......25 G1
Hall La *NHMKT* IP6...........11 H1
Hall Pond Wy *FX* IP11........42 C5
Hall Rd *FRAM/WMKT* IP13......21 F5
KIR/NAC IP10..........27 F4
SMKT IP14.............4 C1
Halls Drift *KESG* IP5........26 D7
Hall Wk *RIPW* IP8............16 C1
Halton Crs *IPSE* IP3.........25 H6
Hamblin Rd *WDBR* IP12........15 J1
Hamilton Gdns *FX* IP11.......53 J2
Hamilton Rd *FX* IP11.........43 F6
IPSE IP3..............25 G6
Hamilton St *FX* IP11.........42 D7
Hamilton Wy *SMKT* IP14........4 E2
Hampton Rd *IP* IP1...........17 J6
Handford Cut *IP* IP1..........2 A3
Handford Rd *IP* IP1...........2 A3
Ha'Penny Fld *RIPS/CAP* IP9...49 F1
Harbour Crs *HAR* CO12........52 A5
Hardwick Cl *FX* IP11.........42 K5
Hardy Cl *MGTR* CO11.........46 C6
Hardy Crs *IP* IP1............17 J7
Harebell Rd *CHTY* IP2........23 J5
Hargrave Av *NHMKT* IP6........6 E6
Harkstead Rd *RIPS/CAP* IP9...49 H1
Harrier Cl *IPSE* IP3.........25 G6
Harrier Wy *SMKT* IP14.........5 H3
Harrison Cv *KESG* IP5........20 D7
Harrow Cl *IPNE* IP4..........25 F2
Hartest Wy *SMKT* IP14.........5 G4
Hartley St *CHTY* IP2.........24 B4
Hartree Wy *KESG* IP5.........21 F5
Harvest Ct *FX* IP11 *........43 G6
Harvesters Wy *KESG* IP5......27 H2
Hasketon Rd *FRAM/WMKT* IP13..13 K3
WDBR IP12.............15 F1
Haskins Wk *KESG* IP5.........21 F6
Haslemere Dr *IPNE* IP4........3 J1
Hatfield Rd *IPSE* IP3........25 F6
Haughgate Cl *WDBR* IP12......15 G3
Haugh La *WDBR* IP12..........15 G2
Haughley Dr *IPNE* IP4........26 A4
Hauliers Rd *FX* IP11.........53 F1
Haven Cl *FX* IP11............42 C6
Haven Ex *FX* IP11 *..........53 F1
The Havens *IPSE* IP3.........33 K1
Hawbridge *RIPS/CAP* IP9......38 E2
Hawes St *CHTY* IP2...........24 C4
Hawker Dr *KESG* IP5..........21 J7
Hawke Rd *FX* IP11............24 D6
Hawkes La *FX* IP11...........42 C6
Hawks Mill St *NHMKT* IP6......6 C1
Hawthorn Cl *SMKT* IP14........5 H4
Hawthorn Dr *CHTY* IP2........23 F7
Hawthorn Pl *WDBR* IP12.......15 F4
Hayhill Rd *IPNE* IP4..........3 H4
Hayman Rd *IPSE* IP3..........24 D4
Haywards Flds *KESG* IP5......20 E6
Hazelcroft Rd *IP* IP1........18 A4
Hazel Dr *IPSE* IP3...........25 K6
Hazelnut Cl *KESG* IP5........19 K5
Hazel Ri *NHMKT* IP6..........11 F7
Hazlitt Rd *IP* IP1...........17 K6
Headingham Cl *CHTY* IP2......23 K4
Heath Cl *RCOLE* CO7..........45 H4
Heath Ct *FX* IP11............36 E6
Heather Av *IPSE* IP3.........25 H6
Heather Cl *KESG* IP5.........27 G2
Heathercroft Rd *IP* IP1......17 K4
Heatherhayes *CHTY* IP2.......24 A4
Heathfield *KESG* IP5.........27 H1
Heathfield Ms *KESG* IP5......27 G1
Heathfield Rd *RIPS/CAP* IP9..49 F2
Heathfields *FX* IP11.........36 D7
Heathgate Piece *FX* IP11.....42 B5
Heathlands Pk *IPNE* IP4......25 K1
Heath La *IPNE* IP4...........25 H1

eath Rd *IPNE* IP4 25 H1
RCOLE CO7 45 H2
eath Vw *KESG* IP5 26 B1
elena Rd *IPSE* IP3 3 H7
elston Cl *KESG* IP5 26 C1
enderson Cl *RIPW* IP8 16 D4
engrave Cl *CHTY* IP2 23 K5
ening Av *IPSE* IP3 33 J1
enley Av *IP* IP1 18 A2
enley Rd *IP* IP1 18 A2
enniker Rd *IP* IP1 17 G5
enry Rd *IPSE* IP3 25 G6
enslow Rd *IPNE* IP4 25 G2
enstead Gdns *IPSE* IP3 25 F5
erbert Rd *KESG* IP5 21 F5
eron Cl *SMKT* IP14 4 B3
eron Rd *CHTY* IP2 23 H4
ervey Cl *RIPS/CAP* IP9 51 G4
ervey St *IPNE* IP4 3 G1
essett Cl *SMKT* IP14 5 G6
eywood Cl *CHTY* IP2 23 G6
ibbard Rd *RIPW* IP8 17 F3
iggins Pl *KESG* IP5 * 21 H6
igham Rd *RCOLE* CO7 44 A2
igh Beach *FX* IP11 43 H6
ighfield Ap *IP* IP1 17 J4
ighfield Dr *NHMKT* IP6 11 G2
ighfield Rd *FX* IP11 43 F6
IP IP1 17 H3
SMKT IP14 5 H1
ighfields *RIPS/CAP* IP9 39 J5
igh Hall Cl *FX* IP11 36 D6
ighlands Cl *NHMKT* IP6 6 D4
ighlands Rd *HADL* IP7 29 F5
igh Rd *FX* IP11 36 C5
igh Rd East *FX* IP11 43 G5
igh Rd West *FX* IP11 42 E4
igh Row Fld *FX* IP11 43 H5
igh St *FRAM/WMKT* IP13 8 D3
FX IP11 42 D4
HADL IP7 28 E4
IP IP1 2 D2
NHMKT IP6 6 E4
RCOLE CO7 44 D6
RIPW IP8 22 D1
igh Vw *MGTR* CO11 * 46 C5
igh View Rd *IP* IP1 17 G5
ildabrook Cl *CHTY* IP2 23 H6
illary Cl *IPNE* IP4 25 F2
illcrest Ap *RIPW* IP8 16 E3
ill Farm La *RIPS/CAP* IP9 40 D4
ill Farm Rd *FRAM/WMKT* IP13 13 G1
NHMKT IP6 20 C1
ill House Cots *FX* IP11 * 42 E3
ill House La *NHMKT* IP6 6 D4
ill House Rd *IPSE* IP3 3 J5
ill Ri *SMKT* IP14 4 E6
ills Cots *RCOLE* CO7 * 44 B3
illside *SMKT* IP14 4 E6
illside Crs *IPSE* IP3 25 G4
ill View Ter *WDBR* IP12 * 15 H4
illy Flds *WDBR* IP12 15 F6
ilton Rd *IPSE* IP3 25 H6
KESG IP5 21 K5
ines Rd *IPSE* IP3 25 F3
intesham Cl *IPNE* IP4 26 A2
intlesham Cl *SMKT* IP14 5 F6
intlesham Dr *FX* IP11 42 C5
iston Cl *KESG* IP5 20 A6
ockney Gdns *IPSE* IP3 33 F1
odgkinson Rd *FX* IP11 52 E1
ogarth Rd *IPSE* IP3 24 E6
ogarth Sq *IPSE* IP3 24 E6
olbecks La *HADL* IP7 28 D6
olbrook Crs *FX* IP11 42 C6
olbrook Rd *IPSE* IP3 24 D6
RIPS/CAP IP9 48 C5
RIPS/CAP IP9 49 J5
olcombe Crs *CHTY* IP2 23 G5
olfen Cl *WDBR* IP12 21 K3
olkham Cl *IPNE* IP4 26 A2
olland Rd *FX* IP11 53 H1
IPNE IP4 24 E1
ollingsworth Rd *SMKT* IP14 5 F4
ollow La *RIPS/CAP* IP9 40 D4
ollow Rd *RIPW* IP8 30 A1
olly Blue Cl *RIPW* IP8 31 H1
ollybush Dr *FX* IP11 43 J3
olly Cl *IPSE* IP3 26 A6
ollycroft Cl *IP* IP1 17 K2
olly End *KESG* IP5 27 G1
olly La *KESG* IP5 19 K3
RIPS/CAP IP9 48 A4
RIPW IP8 31 F1
olly Rd *IP* IP1 18 A6
KESG IP5 20 A6
olm Ct *KESG* IP5 * 20 E5
olst Md *SMKT* IP14 4 D1
olt's La *NHMKT* IP6 7 G3

Holyrood Cl *CHTY* IP2 23 J5
Holywells Cl *IPSE* IP3 3 J7
Holy Wells Rd *IPSE* IP3 24 D4
Homefield *RIPS/CAP* IP9 39 F2
Homer Cl *IP* IP1 17 J1
Homesdale Vls *RIPS/CAP* IP9 * 50 E2
Honeysuckle Gdns *CHTY* IP2 23 H3
Hood Dr *NHMKT* IP6 10 C1
Hood Rd *IPSE* IP3 24 D6
Hook La *HADL* IP7 29 G6
Hope Crs *WDBR* IP12 15 H3
Hop Meadow *RCOLE* CO7 45 F3
Hornbeam Rd *SMKT* IP14 5 H1
Horsham Av *IPSE* IP3 25 K4
Hossack Rd *IPSE* IP3 33 F1
Houghton Pl *IPNE* IP4 26 A2
Howard St *IPNE* IP4 19 G6
Howards Wy *KESG* IP5 21 F5
Howe Av *IPSE* IP3 25 H4
Howlett Cl *KESG* IP5 21 F6
Hoxne Cl *SMKT* IP14 5 F6
Huckleberry Crs *IPSE* IP3 33 H2
Hughes Rd *RCOLE* CO7 44 E1
Humber Doucy La *IPNE* IP4 19 F3
Hunt Cl *SMKT* IP14 4 E6
Hunter Rd *IPSE* IP3 33 H1
Hunters End *FX* IP11 42 B3
Hunters Ride *KESG* IP5 21 J6
Hurdle Makers Hl *RIPW* IP8 22 A3
Hurricane Pl *IPSE* IP3 25 H6
Hurstlea Rd *NHMKT* IP6 6 D4
Hutland Rd *IPNE* IP4 18 E6
Hyams La *RIPS/CAP* IP9 48 E2
Hyam's La *RIPS/CAP* IP9 48 C5
Hyem's La *FX* IP11 43 G3
Hyntle Cl *CHTY* IP2 23 H2

I

Ickworth Ct *FX* IP11 52 E1
Ickworth Crs *IPNE* IP4 26 A2
Iliffe Wy *SMKT* IP14 4 E3
Inglelow Gdns *IPNE* IP4 25 G1
Inkerman Cl *HADL* IP7 28 E4
Inkerman Ter *HADL* IP7 28 E4
Innocence La *KIR/NAC* IP10 36 B3
Inverness Rd *IPNE* IP4 19 F3
Ipswich Rd *FRAM/WMKT* IP13 13 H4
HADL IP7 29 G2
KIR/NAC IP10 34 A3
KIR/NAC IP10 27 K3
MGTR CO11 46 D4
NHMKT IP6 7 F5
RCOLE CO7 44 A5
RIPS/CAP IP9 49 K3
SMKT IP14 5 F5
WDBR IP12 14 E6
Ipswich St *SMKT* IP14 4 E3
Ireland Rd *IPSE* IP3 24 E6
Iris Cl *CHTY* IP2 23 J2
Irlam Rd *CHTY* IP2 23 G5
The Island *RCOLE* CO7 * 44 A5
Ivry St *IP* IP1 18 A6
Ivy Lodge Rd *FRAM/WMKT* IP13 9 K3
Ivy Vls *MGTR* CO11 * 46 D4

J

Jack's Green Rd *NHMKT* IP6 6 E2
Jacksnipe Cl *SMKT* IP14 5 G3
Jackson Cl *KESG* IP5 21 G6
Jackson Ct *KESG* IP5 * 21 H6
Jackson Wy *NHMKT* IP6 6 E5
Jacob Wy *WDBR* IP12 15 H4
Jacqueline Cl *FRAM/WMKT* IP13 13 J3
Jaguar Cl *IP* IP1 17 F4
James Boden Cl *FX* IP11 * 42 D5
Janebrook Rd *CHTY* IP2 23 H5
Jasmine Cl *CHTY* IP2 23 J4
FX IP11 36 E6
Java Lodge Rd
FRAM/WMKT IP13 8 C6
Jay Dr *SMKT* IP14 5 G2
Jeavons La *KESG* IP5 21 F6
Jefferies Rd *IPNE* IP4 3 H3
Jenners Cl *WDBR* IP12 15 J3
Jennings Drift *KESG* IP5 * 20 E6
Jermyns Cl *RIPS/CAP* IP9 39 F1
Jervis Cl *RIPS/CAP* IP9 49 F2
Jewell Vw *KESG* IP5 20 E6
Jimmy's La *MGTR* CO11 47 F3
Johnson Cl *CHTY* IP2 24 B4
John St *IPSE* IP3 3 H7
John Swain Cl *NHMKT* IP6 6 D4
Jordan Cl *NHMKT* IP6 7 F3
Jordayn Ri *HADL* IP7 29 F4
The Josselyns *FX* IP11 42 B2
Jovian Wy *IP* IP1 17 G6
Jubilee Av *SMKT* IP14 4 E5
Jubilee Cl *FX* IP11 36 E6
NHMKT IP6 11 F2
Jubilee Vls *RIPS/CAP* IP9 * 50 E2
June Av *IP* IP1 18 A3
Jupiter Rd *IPNE* IP4 19 G6

K

Karen Cl *IP* IP1 18 A4
Keats Crs *IP* IP1 17 J2
Kelly Rd *CHTY* IP2 23 H2
Kelvedon Dr *IPNE* IP4 26 A2
Kelvin Rd *IP* IP1 17 J4
Kemball St *IPNE* IP4 25 F2
The Kempsters *FX* IP11 42 C3
Kempton Cl *IP* IP1 17 K2
Kempton Rd *IP* IP1 17 K2
Kemsley Rd *FX* IP11 42 E5
Kennedy Cl *IPNE* IP4 25 F1
Kennels Rd *KIR/NAC* IP10 27 F5
Kensington Rd *IP* IP1 17 K5
SMKT IP14 4 E4
Kentford Rd *FX* IP11 42 B6
Kent Rd *SMKT* IP14 4 D2
Kentwell Cl *IPNE* IP4 26 A3
Kenyon Cl *RCOLE* CO7 44 B4
Kenyon St *CHTY* IP2 2 E7
Kerry Av *IP* IP1 17 G3
Kersey Cl *SMKT* IP14 5 F6
Kersey Rd *FX* IP11 53 F1
Kesteven Rd *CHTY* IP2 2 A7
Kestrel Dr *SMKT* IP14 5 H4
Kestrel Rd *CHTY* IP2 23 G4
Keswick Cl *FX* IP11 43 H4
Kettlebaston Wy *IPNE* IP4 18 C4
Kettle La *NHMKT* IP6 7 H5
Key St *IPNE* IP4 3 F5
Keytes Wy *NHMKT* IP6 10 C1
Khartoum Rd *IPNE* IP4 18 E6
Kildare Av *IP* IP1 17 G3
Kiln Bottom *HADL* IP7 29 F2
King Edward Av
FRAM/WMKT IP13 8 D2
King Edward Rd *IPSE* IP3 25 G4
King Edward VII Dr
RIPS/CAP IP9 51 H5
Kingfisher Av *CHTY* IP2 23 G4
Kingfisher Dr *NHMKT* IP6 10 C1
Kingfisher Wy *SMKT* IP14 5 J4
Kings Av *IPNE* IP4 3 H4
Kingsbury Rd *FX* IP11 42 B3
King's Cl *WDBR* IP12 15 F5
Kingsfield Av *IP* IP1 18 C4
Kings Fleet Rd *FX* IP11 53 G1
Kingsgate Dr *IPNE* IP4 18 E5
Kingsland *RIPS/CAP* IP9 50 E3
Kingsley Cl *IP* IP1 17 K2
Kingsmead Cl *SMKT* IP14 4 D2
Kings Quay St *HAR* CO12 52 A4
Kingston Farm Rd *WDBR* IP12 15 G6
Kingston Rd *IP* IP1 17 J5
WDBR IP12 15 H5
King St *FX* IP11 42 D5
IP IP1 2 D3
King's Wy *IPSE* IP3 25 G5
Kingsway *WDBR* IP12 15 J4
King William St *NHMKT* IP6 6 E4
Kinross Rd *IPNE* IP4 19 G4
Kinsey Vw *KESG* IP5 26 C1
Kipling Rd *IP* IP1 17 J2
Kipling Wy *SMKT* IP14 4 C1
Kirby Cl *IPNE* IP4 19 F6
Kirby St *IPNE* IP4 19 F6
Kirkham Cl *CHTY* IP2 23 K5
Kirkton Cl *RIPS/CAP* IP9 51 G4
Kirton Rd *FX* IP11 36 E5
Kitchener Rd *IP* IP1 17 J5
Kitchener Wy *RIPS/CAP* IP9 51 G5
Kittiwake Cl *CHTY* IP2 23 H4
Knights Cl *FX* IP11 43 J4
Knightsdale Rd *IP* IP1 17 K4
Knights La *KESG* IP5 20 E6
Knutsford Cl *RIPW* IP8 23 F6

L

Laburnum Cl *IPSE* IP3 25 K5
RIPW IP8 23 F5
Laburnum Gdns *KESG* IP5 19 K4
Lacewing Cl *RIPW* IP8 31 H1
Lacey St *IPNE* IP4 3 H2
Lacon Rd *RIPW* IP8 16 D3
Lady La *HADL* IP7 29 G3
IP IP1 2 C3
Lady Margaret Gdns *WDBR* IP12 14 E5
Ladywood Rd *IPNE* IP4 19 H6
Lagonda Drive *IP* IP1 17 F3
Lake Side *SMKT* IP14 4 D3
Lakeside Rd *CHTY* IP2 23 H5
Lambert Cl *HADL* IP7 28 E3
Lamberts La *KESG* IP5 19 H3
Lambeth Cl *IP* IP1 17 J5
Lambourne Rd *IP* IP1 18 A1
Lanark Rd *IPNE* IP4 19 G4
Lancaster Dr *KESG* IP5 27 J1
Lancaster Rd *IPNE* IP4 3 H3
Lancaster Wy *NHMKT* IP6 11 F2
The Lancers *WDBR* IP12 14 E6
Lancing Av *IPNE* IP4 19 F5
Landguard Rd *FX* IP11 53 G4
Landseer Cl *IPSE* IP3 25 F6
Landseer Rd *IPSE* IP3 24 E6
Lanercost Wy *CHTY* IP2 23 K6
Langdale Cl *FX* IP11 43 J4
Langer Rd *FX* IP11 53 G3
Langford Cl *SMKT* IP14 4 C1
Langley Av *FX* IP11 42 D6
Langley Cl *FX* IP11 42 D5
Langstons *FX* IP11 42 C2
Lansdowne Rd *FX* IP11 43 G4
IPNE IP4 25 F2
Lapwing Rd *CHTY* IP2 23 G4
Larchcroft Cl *IP* IP1 18 A3
Larchcroft Rd *IP* IP1 18 A3
Larchwood Cl *CHTY* IP2 23 F2
Largent Gv *KESG* IP5 21 F5
Lark Cl *SMKT* IP14 5 H4
Larkhill Ri *IPNE* IP4 25 K2
Larkhill Wy *FX* IP11 42 C5
Larksfield Rd *RIPS/CAP* IP9 48 C4
Larkspur Rd *CHTY* IP2 23 J4
Larksway *FX* IP11 53 F1
La Salle Cl *CHTY* IP2 24 A4
Lattice Av *IPNE* IP4 25 H1
Lattinford Br *RIPS/CAP* IP9 * 38 C4
Laud Ms *IPSE* IP3 25 F5
Laud's Cl *FX* IP11 42 A2
Laurel Av *KESG* IP5 20 B6
Laurel Cots *FX* IP11 * 43 H2
Laurel Dr *NHMKT* IP6 10 D1
Laurelhayes *CHTY* IP2 23 K4
Laurel Wy *NHMKT* IP6 11 F3
Lavender Hl *CHTY* IP2 23 J3
Lavenham Rd *CHTY* IP2 23 H2
Lavenham Wy *SMKT* IP14 5 F5
The Lawns *IPNE* IP4 19 H5
Lawn Wy *FX* IP11 42 D5
Layham Gdns *SMKT* IP14 5 G6
Layham Rd *HADL* IP7 28 E6
Leeks Cl *HADL* IP7 28 E3
Leeks Hl *WDBR* IP12 15 H2
Lee Rd *IPSE* IP3 24 E4
Leeward Ct *FX* IP11 * 43 F5
Leggatt Dr *RIPW* IP8 16 D3
Leicester Cl *CHTY* IP2 23 J6
Leighton Rd *IPSE* IP3 33 F1
Leighton Sq *IPSE* IP3 33 F1
Lely Rd *IPSE* IP3 32 E1
Leopold Gdns *IPNE* IP4 19 F5
Leopold Rd *FX* IP11 43 F6
IPNE IP4 19 F6
Leslie Rd *IPSE* IP3 25 H6
Letton Cl *RIPS/CAP* IP9 38 E2
Levington La *KIR/NAC* IP10 35 H3
Levington Rd *FX* IP11 53 G3
IPSE IP3 25 F3
KIR/NAC IP10 34 D5
Lewes Cl *IPSE* IP3 25 K4
Lewis La *RIPS/CAP* IP9 47 K3
Lidgate Ct *FX* IP11 42 B6
Lilac Wk *NHMKT* IP6 6 E6
Lime Cl *FRAM/WMKT* IP13 8 D3
Limecroft Cl *IP* IP1 17 K2
Limekiln Cl *NHMKT* IP6 11 F3
Lime Kiln Quay Rd *WDBR* IP12 15 J4
Limerick Cl *IP* IP1 17 H3
Limes Av *RIPW* IP8 17 F3
The Limes *KESG* IP5 19 J4
Limetree Cl *NHMKT* IP6 7 F5
Lime Tree Pl *SMKT* IP14 5 F4
Lincoln Cl *IP* IP1 18 A2
Lincoln Gdns *NHMKT* IP6 11 F2
Lincoln Ter *FX* IP11 53 H1
Lindbergh Rd *IPSE* IP3 25 H6
Lindisfarne Cl *CHTY* IP2 23 K6
Lindsey Rd *IPNE* IP4 19 H6
Lindsey Wy *SMKT* IP14 5 F6
Lingfield Rd *IP* IP1 18 A1
Lingside *KESG* IP5 27 G1
Ling's La *RIPS/CAP* IP9 40 B6

Link La *RIPS/CAP* IP9 ....39 H5
Link Rd *RIPS/CAP* IP9 ....38 E2
   RIPS/CAP IP9 ....51 G4
Links Av *FX* IP11 ....43 F4
Linksfield *KESG* IP5 ....19 K6
Linksfield Gdns *KESG* IP5 ....19 K6
The Link *RIPS/CAP* IP9 ....39 H5
Linnet Dr *SMKT* IP14 ....5 H4
Linnet Rd *CHTY* IP2 ....23 G3
Lion La *NHMKT* IP6 ....7 F6
Lion St *IP* IP1 ....2 D3
Lister Rd *HADL* IP7 ....29 G5
   IP IP1 ....17 J4
Little Croft St *CHTY* IP2 ....24 B4
Little Gipping St *IP* IP1 ....2 C3
Little Gv *RIPS/CAP* IP9 ....38 E3
Little Gulls *RIPS/CAP* IP9 ....38 E2
Little Orchards *RIPS/CAP* IP9 ....49 F2
Little St John's St *WDBR* IP12 ....15 J4
Little's Crs *CHTY* IP2 ....2 E7
Little Tufts *RIPS/CAP* IP9 ....39 F2
Little Whip St *CHTY* IP2 ....2 E6
Llewellyn Drift *KESG* IP5 ....20 D6
Lloyd Rd *RIPS/CAP* IP9 ....51 G5
Lloyds Av *IP* IP1 ....2 E3
The Lloyds *KESG* IP5 ....20 D6
Locarno Rd *IPSE* IP3 ....25 G4
Lockington Cl *SMKT* IP14 ....5 F4
Lockington Crs *SMKT* IP14 ....4 E4
Lockington Rd *SMKT* IP14 ....4 E4
Lockwood Cl *IPSE* IP3 ....25 H4
Lodge Farm Dr *FX* IP11 ....43 H5
Lodge La *NHMKT* IP6 ....10 D3
Lodge Rd *FRAM/WMKT* IP13 ....14 A6
Loganberry Rd *IPSE* IP3 ....33 H2
Lombardy Pk *CHTY* IP2 ....24 A6
London Rd *CHTY* IP2 ....23 K1
   IP IP1 ....23 K1
   RIPS/CAP IP9 ....39 F3
   RIPW IP8 ....30 C1
Lone Barn Ct *IP* IP1 ....17 J5
Long Bessels *HADL* IP7 ....28 E4
Longcroft *FX* IP11 ....42 D4
Long Fld *FX* IP11 ....42 C4
Longfield Rd *RIPS/CAP* IP9 ....38 E1
Long Perry *RIPS/CAP* IP9 ....39 F2
Long St *IPSE* IP3 ....3 H5
Lonsdale Cl *IPNE* IP4 ....18 E6
Looe Rd *FX* IP11 ....43 H5
Loraine Wy *RIPW* IP8 ....16 C1
Lotus Cl *IP* IP1 ....17 F4
Loudham Hall Rd
   FRAM/WMKT IP13 ....8 D5
Lovetofts Dr *IP* IP1 ....17 G4
Lower Brook St *IPNE* IP4 ....2 E4
Lower Dales View Rd *IP* IP1 ....17 K5
Lower Falkenham Rd
   KIR/NAC IP10 ....37 H4
Lower Harlings *RIPS/CAP* IP9 ....51 G5
Lower Orwell St *IPNE* IP4 ....3 F5
Lower *FRAM/WMKT* IP13 ....14 A4
   KIR/NAC IP10 ....37 J5
   NHMKT IP6 ....18 C1
Lower St *FRAM/WMKT* IP13 ....8 E2
   NHMKT IP6 ....7 G6
   RCOLE CO7 ....44 A4
   RIPS/CAP IP9 ....40 C4
   RIPW IP8 ....16 D6
Low Rd *FRAM/WMKT* IP13 ....14 C1
Lowry Gdns *IPSE* IP3 ....33 F1
Lowry Wy *SMKT* IP14 ....4 C3
Lucena Ct *SMKT* IP14 ....4 D3
Ludbrook Cl *NHMKT* IP6 ....6 D4
Ludlow Cl *IP* IP1 ....18 A1
Luff Meadow *NHMKT* IP6 ....6 E4
Lugano Av *KESG* IP5 ....21 K5
Lulworth Av *IPSE* IP3 ....25 J4
Lummis V *KESG* IP5 ....20 D6
Lupin Rd *CHTY* IP2 ....23 H3
Lupin Wy *NHMKT* IP6 ....6 E2
Luther Rd *CHTY* IP2 ....2 C7
Lydgate Rd *SMKT* IP14 ....4 C2
Lyle Cl *KESG* IP5 ....21 F6
Lyndhurst Av *IPNE* IP4 ....25 H2
Lynwood Av *FX* IP11 ....43 G5
Lysander Dr *IPSE* IP3 ....33 H1

M

Macaulay Rd *IP* IP1 ....17 J1
Mackenzie Dr *KESG* IP5 ....20 C5
Magdalen Dr *WDBR* IP12 ....14 E6
Magdalene Cl *CHTY* IP2 ....23 J5
Magdalene Rd *HADL* IP7 ....28 E4
Magingley Crs *KESG* IP5 ....26 A1
Magpie Cl *RIPW* IP8 ....23 F5
Maidenhall Ap *CHTY* IP2 ....24 A5

Maidstone Rd *FX* IP11 ....42 D5
Main Rd *FRAM/WMKT* IP13 ....8 E1
   HAR CO12 ....52 A5
   IPNE IP4 ....19 F2
   KESG IP5 ....20 B5
   KIR/NAC IP10 ....27 G6
   RIPS/CAP IP9 ....40 A3
   WDBR IP12 ....21 H4
Maitland Rd *NHMKT* IP6 ....7 F6
Mallard Wy *CHTY* IP2 ....23 H5
   SMKT IP14 ....4 B3
Mallowhayes Cl *CHTY* IP2 ....24 A4
Malmesbury Cl *CHTY* IP2 ....23 K5
Malting La *FRAM/WMKT* IP13 ....13 H5
Malting Ter *CHTY* IP2 * 3 F7
Malvern Cl *IPSE* IP3 ....25 G3
   KESG IP5 ....20 A6
Malyon Rd *HADL* IP7 ....29 F2
Manchester Rd *CHTY* IP2 ....23 G5
Mandy Cl *IPNE* IP4 ....25 F1
Mannall Wk *KESG* IP5 ....21 F5
Manning Rd *FX* IP11 ....53 H2
Mannington Cl *IPNE* IP4 ....26 A2
Manningtree Rd *RCOLE* CO7 ....45 K4
Manor La *RIPS/CAP* IP9 ....48 A5
Manor Rd *FRAM/WMKT* IP13 ....14 E3
   FX IP11 ....42 A2
   FX IP11 ....53 G3
   IPNE IP4 ....18 C5
   KESG IP5 ....21 H5
Manor Ter *FX* IP11 ....53 G4
Mansbrook Bvd *CHTY* IP2 ....33 J2
Mansfield Av *IP* IP1 ....17 J3
Manthorp Cl *WDBR* IP12 ....15 J1
Manwick Rd *FX* IP11 ....53 G2
Maple Cl *CHTY* IP2 ....23 K4
Maple Rd *SMKT* IP14 ....5 H1
The Maples *IPNE* IP4 ....19 K5
Marbled White Dr *RIPW* IP8 ....31 H1
Marcus Rd *FX* IP11 ....43 J5
Margaret Rd *SMKT* IP14 ....4 D1
Margaret St *FX* IP11 ....42 D5
Margate Rd *IPSE* IP3 ....25 G4
Margery Girling House *FX* IP11 * 43 H4
Marigold Av *CHTY* IP2 ....23 H4
Marina Gdns *FX* IP11 ....53 G2
Market Hl *WDBR* IP12 ....15 G4
Market Pl *HADL* IP7 ....28 E5
Market Rd *IP* IP1 ....2 C4
Market St *HAR* CO12 * 52 A4
Marlborough Rd *IPNE* IP4 ....24 E2
Marlow Rd *IP* IP1 ....17 G4
Marriott's Wk *SMKT* IP14 ....4 E4
Marshall Cl *KESG* IP5 ....20 D5
Marshalls Meadow *SMKT* IP14 ....5 H1
Marsh La *FX* IP11 ....43 J1
Martello La *FX* IP11 ....43 J5
Martinet Gn *IPSE* IP3 ....25 G6
Martin Rd *CHTY* IP2 ....2 D7
Martinsyde *KESG* IP5 ....21 J5
Martlesham Rd
   FRAM/WMKT IP13 ....21 F2
The Marvens *RIPW* IP8 ....22 D6
Maryon Rd *IPSE* IP3 ....33 G1
Masefield Rd *SMKT* IP14 ....4 C1
Mason Ct *NHMKT* IP6 ....10 E2
Masons Cl *IPNE* IP4 ....24 E1
Mather Wy *CHTY* IP2 ....3 F7
Mathews Rd *RCOLE* CO7 ....44 A4
Matlock Cl *CHTY* IP2 ....23 F5
Matson Rd *IP* IP1 ....17 J3
Maude St *IPSE* IP3 ....3 H7
Maudslay Rd *IP* IP1 ....17 F3
Maybury Rd *IPSE* IP3 ....25 G6
Maybush La *FX* IP11 ....43 H5
Maycroft Cl *IP* IP1 ....17 K1
Mayfield La *KESG* IP5 ....27 H1
Mayfield Rd *IPNE* IP4 ....19 H6
Mayfields *KESG* IP5 ....27 H1
Mayflower Av *HAR* CO12 ....52 A5
Mayfly Cl *RIPW* IP8 ....31 H1
May Rd *IPSE* IP3 ....25 H5
Mead Dr *KESG* IP5 ....20 C6
Meadow Cl *FX* IP11 ....36 E6
Meadow Crs *IPSE* IP3 ....26 A6
Meadowlands *KIR/NAC* IP10 ....36 E3
Meadowside *FRAM/WMKT* IP13 ....8 D2
Meadowside Gdns *IPNE* IP4 ....19 K5
Meadows Wy *HADL* IP7 ....28 E4
Meadowvale Cl *IPNE* IP4 ....18 E6
Meadow Vw *KIR/NAC* IP10 ....35 H1
   NHMKT IP6 ....6 D4
Meadow Wk *WDBR* IP12 ....15 F5
Medway Rd *IPSE* IP3 ....24 E5
Meeting La *FRAM/WMKT* IP13 ....13 H3
Melbourne Rd *IPNE* IP4 ....19 J6
Melford Cl *IPNE* IP4 ....26 A2
Melford Rd *SMKT* IP14 ....5 G5

Melford Wy *FX* IP11 ....52 E1
Melplash Cl *IPSE* IP3 ....25 K3
Melplash Rd *IPSE* IP3 ....25 K3
Melrose Gdns *IPNE* IP4 ....19 G5
Melton Grange Rd *WDBR* IP12 ....15 H3
Melton Hl *WDBR* IP12 ....15 J4
Melton Meadow Rd *WDBR* IP12 ....15 J3
Melton Rd *WDBR* IP12 ....15 J3
Melville Rd *IPNE* IP4 ....3 K4
Mendip Dr *KESG* IP5 ....26 A1
Meredith Rd *IP* IP1 ....17 H3
Mere Gdns *IPNE* IP4 ....26 A3
Meriton Ri *HADL* IP7 ....29 G6
Merion Cl *IPSE* IP3 ....23 F4
Merriam Cl *MGTR* CO11 ....46 D5
Merrion Cl *CHTY* IP2 ....23 F5
Mersey Rd *IPSE* IP3 ....24 E4
Michigan Cl *KESG* IP5 ....20 C6
Mickfield Ms *FX* IP11 ....42 C5
Micklegate Rd *FX* IP11 ....53 G3
Middleton Cl *CHTY* IP2 ....23 G5
Middleton Rd *NHMKT* IP6 ....11 F2
Milden Cl *SMKT* IP14 ....5 F6
Milden Rd *CHTY* IP2 ....23 H2
Mildmay Rd *IPSE* IP3 ....25 F6
Mill Cl *FX* IP11 ....42 C6
   FX IP11 ....36 D6
   RIPS/CAP IP9 ....38 C2
Millers Cl *HADL* IP7 ....29 F4
Millers Ct *SMKT* IP14 ....4 D6
Millers Cl *NHMKT* IP6 ....10 E2
Millers Vw *IP* IP1 ....17 J6
Millfield *RIPS/CAP* IP9 * 40 C4
Mill Fld *RIPW* IP8 ....16 E3
Millfield Av *SMKT* IP14 ....4 D4
Millfield Gdns *IPNE* IP4 ....19 F6
Mill Hl *FRAM/WMKT* IP13 ....13 J2
   RIPS/CAP IP9 ....38 C2
Mill La *FRAM/WMKT* IP13 ....14 B2
   FRAM/WMKT IP13 ....8 D3
   FX IP11 ....42 D6
   FX IP11 ....36 D6
   HADL IP7 ....28 A1
   NHMKT IP6 ....6 E1
   NHMKT IP6 ....6 E1
   RCOLE CO7 ....44 A4
   RIPS/CAP IP9 ....40 C4
   RIPW IP8 ....22 C6
   RIPW IP8 ....16 E4
   WDBR IP12 ....15 H4
Mill Piece *KIR/NAC* IP10 ....34 C3
Mill Pouch *FX* IP11 ....42 A2
Mill Ri *RIPS/CAP* IP9 ....49 F2
Mill Rd *RCOLE* CO7 ....44 B3
Mill Road Dr *IPSE* IP3 ....26 A6
The Mills *IPNE* IP4 ....19 K5
Mill St *SMKT* IP14 ....5 J2
Mill View Cl *WDBR* IP12 ....15 F4
Milner St *IPNE* IP4 ....3 H4
Milton Rd East *SMKT* IP14 ....5 F3
Milton Rd North *SMKT* IP14 ....5 F3
Milton Rd South *SMKT* IP14 ....5 F3
Milton St *IPNE* IP4 ....19 F6
Minos Wy *IP* IP1 ....17 G5
Minsmere Rd *IPSE* IP3 ....33 J1
Mission La *RCOLE* CO7 ....46 B2
Mistley Wy *WDBR* IP12 ....15 G3
Mitford Cl *IP* IP1 ....17 K1
Mitre Wy *IPSE* IP3 ....3 J6
Moat Farm Cl *IPNE* IP4 ....18 E5
Moffat Av *IPNE* IP4 ....19 G4
Monks Cl *FX* IP11 ....43 J4
Monks Ga *RIPW* IP8 ....22 D1
Monmouth Cl *CHTY* IP2 ....24 A6
Monro Rd *FX* IP11 ....43 H5
Montana Rd *KESG* IP5 ....20 B6
Montgomery Rd *CHTY* IP2 ....23 H5
Monton Ri *CHTY* IP2 ....23 G5
Monument Farm Rd
   KIR/NAC IP10 ....26 D4
Moore Rd *IP* IP1 ....17 J2
Moorfield Cl *KESG* IP5 ....20 D6
Moorfield Rd *WDBR* IP12 ....15 F4
Moor's Wy *WDBR* IP12 ....15 H4
Morgan Ct *NHMKT* IP6 ....11 F3
Morgan Dr *IP* IP1 ....17 F3
Morland Rd *IPSE* IP3 ....33 F1
Morley Av *WDBR* IP12 ....15 G5
Mornington Av *IP* IP1 ....17 J4
Morris Wy *NHMKT* IP6 ....6 E5
Mors End *RCOLE* CO7 ....44 B3
Morston Hall Rd *FX* IP11 ....36 B5
Moss La *NHMKT* IP6 ....18 E1
Mottram Ct *IP* IP1 ....17 F3
Mountbatten Ct *IP* IP1 ....2 A1
Mount Dr *IPSE* IP3 ....25 G5
Mowlands *RIPS/CAP* IP9 ....39 F2
Mulberry Gdns *NHMKT* IP6 ....10 D1

Mulberry Rd *IPSE* IP3 ....33 H
Mumford Rd *IP* IP1 ....17 H
Munnings Cl *IPSE* IP3 ....33 C
Muriel Cl *HADL* IP7 ....29 F
Murray Rd *IPSE* IP3 ....25 F
Murrills Rd *IPSE* IP3 ....26 A
Museum St *IP* IP1 ....2 D
Mussiden Pl *WDBR* IP12 * ....15 C
Myrtle Rd *IPSE* IP3 3

N

Nacton Crs *IPSE* IP3 ....25 C
Nacton Rd *FX* IP11 ....53 C
   IPSE IP3 ....33 H
   IPSE IP3 ....3 K
   KIR/NAC IP10 ....33 K
Nansen Rd *IPSE* IP3 ....25 C
Naughton Gdns *SMKT* IP14 ....5 F
Naunton Rd *WDBR* IP12 ....15 H
Navarre St *IP* IP1 ....2 E
Naverne Meadow *WDBR* IP12 ....15 H
Nayland Rd *FX* IP11 ....52 E
Neale St *IP* IP1 ....2 E
Neath Dr *IPSE* IP3 ....23 H
Needham Rd *SMKT* IP14 ....5 F
Nelson Rd *IPNE* IP4 ....19 H
Nelson Wy *WDBR* IP12 ....15 C
Nene Dr *IPSE* IP3 ....33 .
Neptune Quay *IPNE* IP4 ....3 C
Neptune Sq *IPNE* IP4 ....3 C
Ness Rd *RIPS/CAP* IP9 ....50 A
Netley Cl *IPSE* IP3 ....31 .
Newark Cl *CHTY* IP2 ....23 .
Newbourne Gdns *FX* IP11 ....53 F
Newbourne Rd *KIR/NAC* IP10 ....27 .
Newbury Rd *IPNE* IP4 ....25 C
Newby Dr *IPNE* IP4 ....26 A
New Cardinal St *IP* IP1 ....2 C
New Cots *MGTR* CO11 * ....46 E
New Cut *HADL* IP7 ....29 F
Newell Ri *NHMKT* IP6 ....11 F
Newhaven Wy *HADL* IP7 ....29 F
New La *RIPS/CAP* IP9 ....49 F
Newmill La *MGTR* CO11 ....47 C
Newnham Av *WDBR* IP12 ....14 E
Newnham Ct *CHTY* IP2 ....23 H
Newquay Cl *KESG* IP5 ....26 A
New Quay La *WDBR* IP12 ....15 .
New Rd *FX* IP11 ....42 E
Newry Av *FX* IP11 ....42 E
Newson St *IP* IP1 ....2 C
New St *IPNE* IP4 ....3 C
   WDBR IP12 ....15 H
Newton Rd *IPSE* IP3 ....25 F
   SMKT IP14 ....5 F
Newton St *IPNE* IP4 ....3 C
New Wy *CHTY* IP2 ....23 .
Nicholas Rd *FX* IP11 ....42 E
Nightingale Cl *SMKT* IP14 ....5 F
Nightingale Rd *IPSE* IP3 ....33 H
Nightingale Sq *IPSE* IP3 ....33 H
Nine Acres *IPSE* IP3 ....23 C
Nock Gdns *KESG* IP5 ....26 A
Norbury Rd *IPNE* IP4 ....19 C
Norfolk Rd *IPNE* IP4 ....3 C
Norman Cl *FX* IP11 ....43 .
   WDBR IP12 ....15 H
Norman Crs *IPSE* IP3 ....25 F
Normandy Cl *SMKT* IP14 ....4 E
North Cl *IPNE* IP4 ....18 E
Northgate St *IP* IP1 ....2 E
North Hl *WDBR* IP12 ....15 C
North Hill Gdns *IPNE* IP4 ....3 .
North Hill Rd *IPNE* IP4 ....3 .
North Lawn *IPNE* IP4 ....19 C
North Quay *FX* IP11 * ....52 E
Norwich Rd *IP* IP1 ....2 A
   NHMKT IP6 ....10 E
   NHMKT IP6 ....7 .
Notcutts *RCOLE* CO7 ....45 .
Nottidge Rd *IPNE* IP4 ....3 .
Nunn Cl *WDBR* IP12 ....21 H
Nursery Wk *FX* IP11 ....42 E

O

Oak Cl *FX* IP11 ....42 D
Oakdene *KIR/NAC* IP10 ....36 E
Oakfield Rd *RIPW* IP8 ....30 C
Oak Gv *RIPW* IP8 ....22 D
Oak Hill La *CHTY* IP2 ....24 A
Oaklee *CHTY* IP2 ....23 H
Oak Rd *SMKT* IP14 ....5 H
Oaksmere Gdns *CHTY* IP2 ....23 C

akstead Cl *IPNE* IP4 .... 24 E1
ne Oaks *KESG* IP5 .... 27 G1
ban St *IP* IP1 .... 2 B1
fford Cl *KESG* IP5 .... 26 F1
ld Barrack Rd *WDBR* IP12 .... 14 E6
ld Cattle Market *IPNE* IP4 .... 2 E4
ldfield Rd *RIPW* IP8 .... 22 E6
ld Forge Ms *WDBR* IP12 .... 15 K1
ld Foundry Rd *IPNE* IP4 .... 3 F3
ld Hall Cl *FX* IP11 .... 43 H5
ld Hall La *RIPS/CAP* IP9 .... 30 C6
ldhall Rd *RIPS/CAP* IP9 .... 51 F1
ld Ipswich Rd *NHMKT* IP6 .... 11 F3
ld Kirton Rd *FX* IP11 .... 36 D6
ld London Rd *RIPS/CAP* IP9 .... 38 D4
ne Old Maltings *SMKT* IP14 .... 5 F4
ld Norwich Rd *IP* IP1 .... 17 H1
ld Paper Mill La *NHMKT* IP6 .... 11 F1
ld Rectory Cl *NHMKT* IP6 .... 11 F1
lympus Cl *IP* IP1 .... 17 F3
nehouse La *IP* IP1 .... 18 A4
nehouse Rd *SMKT* IP14 .... 4 C3
pal Av *IP* IP1 .... 17 G4
rchard Cl *WDBR* IP12 .... 15 H2
rchard End *FRAM/WMKT* IP13 .... 13 J3
rchard Gdns *WDBR* IP12 .... 15 J4
rchard Gdns *CHTY* IP2 .... 23 G2
  NHMKT IP6 .... 6 D4
rchard Gv *KESG* IP5 .... 20 B6
  NHMKT IP6 .... 11 F4
rchard Pl *FRAM/WMKT* IP13 .... 13 J4
rchard Rw *FX* IP11 * 42 D5
rchard St *IPNE* IP4 .... 3 F4
rchid Cl *CHTY* IP2 .... 23 H3
rchid Wy *NHMKT* IP6 .... 6 E6
regon Rd *KESG* IP5 .... 26 B1
rford Pl *FX* IP11 .... 53 G3
rford St *IP* IP1 .... 2 B1
rion Av *NHMKT* IP6 .... 10 C3
rkney Rd *IPNE* IP4 .... 19 F4
rvis La *RCOLE* CO7 .... 45 J4
well Br *RIPS/CAP* IP9 .... 32 D2
well Gdns *CHTY* IP2 * 23 K4
well Rd *IP* IP1 .... 3 F4
well Ri *RIPS/CAP* IP9 .... 40 D3
well Rd *FX* IP11 .... 53 H1
  IPSE IP3 .... 25 F3
  SMKT IP14 .... 4 E5
well View Rd *RIPS/CAP* IP9 .... 51 F2
sborne Rd *IPSE* IP3 .... 25 J3
sier Cl *WDBR* IP12 .... 15 J3
e Osiers *SMKT* IP14 .... 4 E4
ley Cl *FX* IP11 .... 42 C5
ulton Rd *FX* IP11 .... 5 F5
tpart Eastward *HAR* CO12 * 52 A4
xford Dr *HADL* IP7 .... 28 E2
  WDBR IP12 .... 14 E6
xford Rd *IPNE* IP4 .... 3 H4
  IPSE IP3 .... 20 B6
sterbed Rd *FX* IP11 .... 52 C1

P

ckard Av *IPSE* IP3 .... 25 G5
ckard Pl *RIPW* IP8 .... 16 E3
e Paddocks *KESG* IP5 .... 21 H5
dstow Rd *KESG* IP5 .... 26 B1
ge Gdns *KESG* IP5 .... 21 F5
ge's Cl *SMKT* IP14 .... 4 D4
get Cl *NHMKT* IP6 .... 6 D4
get Rd *IP* IP1 .... 18 A6
frey Hts *MGTR* CO11 .... 46 D5
imcroft Cl *IP* IP1 .... 17 K2
imcroft Rd *IP* IP1 .... 17 K2
imerston Rd *IPNE* IP4 .... 3 H3
per Mill La *RIPW* IP8 .... 10 E6
rade Rd *IPNE* IP4 .... 3 K1
rdoe Pl *IPNE* IP4 .... 25 K2
rk Av *FX* IP11 .... 43 G5
rk Cl *KESG* IP5 .... 21 H5
rker Av *FX* IP11 .... 52 D1
rkers Rd *IPSE* IP3 .... 21 H5
rkeston Rd *FX* IP11 .... 42 C6
rk Farm Cots *FX* IP11 * 43 H3
rk La *KIR/NAC* IP10 .... 36 E1
rk North *IP* IP1 .... 18 C5
rk Rd *FRAM/WMKT* IP13 .... 13 H4
  IP IP1 .... 18 B5
  NHMKT IP6 .... 6 E4
  RCOLE CO7 .... 46 B3
rk View Rd *IP* IP1 .... 18 A4
rkway *FRAM/WMKT* IP13 .... 8 F1
rliament Rd *IPNE* IP4 .... 25 G2
rnell Cl *IP* IP1 .... 17 J2
rnell Rd *IP* IP1 .... 17 J2

Parnham Pl *IPNE* IP4 .... 26 A2
Parsonage Cl *IP11* 42 C6
Partridge Rd *IPSE* IP3 .... 23 G4
Pashford Pl *IPSE* IP3 .... 33 H1
The Pastures *IPNE* IP4 .... 26 A2
Pattern Bush Cl *MGTR* CO11 .... 46 D5
Patteson Rd *IPSE* IP3 .... 3 H7
Pauline St *CHTY* IP2 .... 24 B4
Paul's Rd *CHTY* IP2 .... 23 J2
Pax Ter *MGTR* CO11 * 46 D4
Peacock St *KESG* IP5 .... 21 F6
Pearce Rd *IPSE* IP3 .... 25 F3
Pearcroft Rd *IP* IP1 .... 18 A2
Pearl Rd *IP* IP1 .... 17 F5
Pearse Wy *IPSE* IP3 .... 25 K6
Pearson Rd *IPSE* IP3 .... 25 H2
Pearsons Wy *RIPW* IP8 .... 22 C6
Peasey Gdns *KESG* IP5 .... 26 D1
Peasey La *KESG* IP5 .... 26 D1
Peel St *IP* IP1 .... 2 D2
Peel Yd *KESG* IP5 .... 21 H5
Peewit Cl *FX* IP11 * 53 F1
Peewit Hl *FX* IP11 .... 53 F1
Peewit Rd *CHTY* IP2 .... 23 F4
Pelican Cl *IPSE* IP3 .... 23 H4
Pembroke Av *WDBR* IP12 .... 15 F5
Pembroke Cl *IPSE* IP3 .... 24 A4
Pendleton Rd *CHTY* IP2 .... 23 G6
Penfold Rd *FX* IP11 .... 43 F6
Penn Cl *RIPS/CAP* IP9 .... 39 F1
Penny La *IPSE* IP3 .... 26 A6
Penny Meadow *RIPS/CAP* IP9 .... 38 E2
Pennyroyal Gdns *CHTY* IP2 .... 23 H3
Penryn Rd *KESG* IP5 .... 20 A6
Penshurst Rd *IPSE* IP3 .... 25 J3
Penzance Rd *KESG* IP5 .... 26 B1
Peppercorn Wy *CHTY* IP2 .... 24 B4
Pepper Pl *KESG* IP5 .... 26 E1
Perkins Wy *IPSE* IP3 .... 24 E6
Peterhouse Cl *CHTY* IP2 .... 23 H5
Peterhouse Crs *WDBR* IP12 .... 14 E5
Peter's Gv *RIPS/CAP* IP9 .... 38 E2
Pheasant Ri *RIPW* IP8 .... 30 C1
Pheasant Rd *CHTY* IP2 .... 23 H4
Philip Av *FX* IP11 .... 53 F1
Philip Rd *IP* IP1 .... 2 D7
Phillipps Rd *NHMKT* IP6 .... 11 F2
Phillips Crs *NHMKT* IP6 .... 7 F5
Phoenix La *IPNE* IP4 .... 19 F6
Phoenix Wy *SMKT* IP14 .... 5 G2
Picketts Rd *FX* IP11 .... 43 H5
Pickwick Rd *CHTY* IP2 .... 23 H1
Picton Av *IP* IP1 .... 18 C4
Pier Rd *FX* IP11 .... 52 E4
Pigeon's La *RIPW* IP8 .... 22 A5
The Pightle *NHMKT* IP6 .... 6 E4
  RIPS/CAP IP9 .... 39 F1
Pimpernel Rd *CHTY* IP2 .... 23 J4
Pine Av *IP* IP1 .... 18 A4
Pine Bank *KESG* IP5 .... 27 G1
Pine Cl *MGTR* CO11 .... 46 D5
Pinecroft Rd *IP* IP1 .... 17 K3
Pinecroft Wy *NHMKT* IP6 .... 7 F5
Pine Gv *FRAM/WMKT* IP13 .... 13 J4
The Pines *FX* IP11 .... 43 K4
  NHMKT IP6 .... 11 F3
Pinetree Cl *KESG* IP5 .... 20 A6
Pineview Cl *SMKT* IP14 .... 4 E4
Pine View Rd *IP* IP1 .... 18 A5
Pinewood *WDBR* IP12 .... 15 F6
Pin Mill Cl *IPSE* IP3 .... 23 F6
Pinmill Rd *RIPS/CAP* IP9 .... 40 D3
Pinners La *FRAM/WMKT* IP13 .... 14 C2
Pintail Cl *CHTY* IP2 .... 23 H5
Pintail Rd *SMKT* IP14 .... 5 H3
Pipers Vale *IPSE* IP3 .... 24 D6
Pitcairn Rd *IP* IP1 .... 17 H5
Pitts End *RCOLE* CO7 .... 45 H2
Platten Cl *NHMKT* IP6 .... 6 D4
Platters Cl *IPSE* IP3 .... 33 F2
Platters Rd *FX* IP11 .... 53 G2
Playfield Rd *NHMKT* IP6 .... 39 F2
Playford La *KESG* IP5 .... 19 K4
Playford Rd *FRAM/WMKT* IP13 .... 20 E3
  IPNE IP4 .... 19 J6
  IPSE IP3 .... 20 B4
Pleasant Rw *IPNE* IP4 .... 3 F5
Plough Rd *RIPS/CAP* IP9 .... 38 D2
Plough St *IPSE* IP3 .... 3 J6
Plover Cl *SMKT* IP14 .... 5 H3
Plover Rd *CHTY* IP2 .... 23 H5
Plummers Dell *NHMKT* IP6 .... 10 D1
Plymouth Rd *FX* IP11 .... 42 E4
Polstead Cl *SMKT* IP14 .... 5 G5
Pond Cl *FX* IP11 .... 53 H1
Pond Hall Rd *HADL* IP7 .... 29 H6
Poole Cl *IPSE* IP3 .... 25 F3
Poplar Cl *NHMKT* IP6 .... 11 F3
Poplar Hl *SMKT* IP14 .... 4 E5

Poplar La *RIPW* IP8 .... 22 E4
The Poplars *MGTR* CO11 .... 46 D3
Poppy Cl *CHTY* IP2 .... 23 J2
Portal Av *KESG* IP5 .... 20 C5
Porter Rd *IPSE* IP3 .... 26 A6
Portland Crs *WDBR* IP12 .... 15 F5
Portman Rd *IP* IP1 .... 2 C3
Port of Felixstowe Rd *FX* IP11 .... 42 B5
Post Mill Cl *FRAM/WMKT* IP13 .... 13 H4
  IPNE IP4 .... 3 K2
Post Mill Crs *FRAM/WMKT* IP13 * 13 H4
Post Mill Gdns *FRAM/WMKT* IP13 .... 13 H4
Post Mill Orch *FRAM/WMKT* IP13 .... 13 H4
Post Office La *WDBR* IP12 .... 21 K1
Potash La *RIPS/CAP* IP9 .... 39 J3
Pound La *HADL* IP7 .... 28 J3
  RIPS/CAP IP9 .... 38 D4
  RIPW IP8 .... 10 B5
  RIPW IP8 .... 30 D2
  SMKT IP14 .... 4 E2
Powling Wy *IPSE* IP3 .... 25 F5
Pownall Rd *IPSE* IP3 .... 3 H6
Prentices La *WDBR* IP12 .... 14 E3
Prentice Wy *IPSE* IP3 .... 25 G6
Presmere Rd *FRAM/WMKT* IP13 .... 8 B5
Preston Dr *IP* IP1 .... 17 J5
Prestwick Av *FX* IP11 .... 43 H4
Pretyman Rd *FX* IP11 .... 53 G3
  IPSE IP3 .... 25 H4
Priestly Cl *SMKT* IP14 .... 4 C1
Priestly Rd *NHMKT* IP6 .... 6 C5
Primrose HI *CHTY* IP2 .... 23 J6
  RIPS/CAP IP9 .... 49 F3
Primrose Wy *NHMKT* IP6 .... 6 E6
Princedale Cl *IP* IP1 .... 17 K4
Princel La *RCOLE* CO7 .... 44 D6
Prince of Wales Dr *CHTY* IP2 .... 23 K5
Princes Gdns *FX* IP11 .... 42 E6
Princes Rd *FX* IP11 .... 53 J1
Princes St *CHTY* IP2 .... 2 B6
Princethorpe Rd *IPSE* IP3 .... 25 H3
Priory Rd *FX* IP11 .... 43 J5
Prittlewell Cl *CHTY* IP2 .... 23 J6
Private Rd *WDBR* IP12 .... 21 J3
The Promenade *FX* IP11 * 42 E2
Prospect Pl *WDBR* IP12 * 15 J3
Prospect Rd *IP* IP1 .... 2 A1
Prospect St *IP* IP1 .... 23 K1
Provan Ct *IPSE* IP3 .... 25 G3
Providence La *IP* IP1 .... 17 K6
Providence St *IP* IP1 .... 2 D3
Puffin Cl *SMKT* IP14 .... 5 H3
Pump St *NHMKT* IP6 .... 7 F5
Punchard Wy *FX* IP11 .... 42 B2
Purdis Av *FX* IP11 .... 26 A6
Purdis Farm La *IPSE* IP3 .... 26 A5
Purdis Rd *KIR/NAC* IP10 .... 26 E5
Purplett St *CHTY* IP2 .... 3 F7
Putticks La *RCOLE* CO7 .... 45 J2
Pykenham Wy *HADL* IP7 .... 28 E4
Pytches Cl *WDBR* IP12 .... 15 H3
Pytches Rd *WDBR* IP12 .... 15 H3

Q

Quail Cl *SMKT* IP14 .... 5 G2
Quantock Cl *KESG* IP5 .... 20 A6
Quantrill Ter *KESG* IP5 .... 26 E1
Quay Side *WDBR* IP12 .... 15 J5
Quay St *WDBR* IP12 .... 15 H5
Quebec Dr *KESG* IP5 .... 20 C5
Queech La *RIPS/CAP* IP9 .... 47 J6
The Queech *RIPS/CAP* IP9 .... 39 F1
Queens Av *WDBR* IP12 .... 15 F5
Queensberry Rd *IPSE* IP3 .... 25 F6
Queenscliffe Rd *CHTY* IP2 .... 23 K4
Queensdale Cl *IP* IP1 .... 18 A4
Queensgate Dr *IPNE* IP4 .... 18 E5
Queen's Head La *WDBR* IP12 .... 15 G4
Queensland *RIPS/CAP* IP9 .... 50 E3
Queen's Rd *FX* IP11 .... 53 J1
Queens Rw *HADL* IP7 * 28 E3
Queen's Sq *IPSE* IP3 .... 25 G5
Queen St *FX* IP11 .... 42 D4
  HADL IP7 .... 28 E4
  IP IP1 .... 2 D4
Queen's Wy *IPSE* IP3 .... 25 G5
Queen Victoria Dr *RIPS/CAP* IP9 .... 51 H5
Quentin Cl *IP* IP1 .... 17 H5
Quilter Dr *RIPW* IP8 .... 23 F6
Quilter Rd *FX* IP11 .... 43 G6
Quince Cl *MGTR* CO11 .... 46 D4
Quinton Rd *NHMKT* IP6 .... 6 D5

Quintons Ct *NHMKT* IP6 * 7 F5
Quinton's La *FX* IP11 .... 43 H5
Quintons Rd *RCOLE* CO7 .... 45 G2
Quoits Fld *NHMKT* IP6 .... 11 F3

R

Radcliffe Dr *CHTY* IP2 .... 23 G5
Raeburn Rd *IPSE* IP3 .... 24 E6
Raeburn Rd South *IPSE* IP3 .... 32 E1
Railway Ap *FX* IP11 .... 43 F5
Rampling Cl *HADL* IP7 .... 28 E3
Ramsey Cl *CHTY* IP2 .... 23 K6
Ramsey Rd *HADL* IP7 .... 29 G3
Ramsgate Dr *IPSE* IP3 .... 25 G4
Randall Cl *KESG* IP5 .... 21 F6
Rands Wy *IPSE* IP3 .... 25 G5
Rand Well Cl *IPNE* IP4 .... 25 G2
Ranelagh Rd *CHTY* IP2 .... 23 K2
  FX IP11 .... 53 J1
Ransome Cl *RIPW* IP8 .... 22 D1
Ransome Crs *IPSE* IP3 .... 25 G5
Ransome Rd *IPSE* IP3 .... 25 G5
Ransomes Wy *IPSE* IP3 .... 25 J6
Ransom Rd *WDBR* IP12 .... 15 F3
Ranson Rd *NHMKT* IP6 .... 6 D4
Rapier St *CHTY* IP2 .... 24 B4
Rattlesden Cl *SMKT* IP14 .... 4 E6
Ravensfield Rd *IP* IP1 .... 17 H3
Ravens La *RIPW* IP8 .... 16 D3
Ravens Wy *WDBR* IP12 .... 21 J3
Ravenswood Av *IPSE* IP3 .... 33 G1
Raven Wy *HADL* IP7 .... 28 E6
Raydon Cft *SMKT* IP14 .... 5 G6
Rayleigh Rd *IP* IP1 .... 17 H4
Rayment Drift *KESG* IP5 .... 20 D6
Reade Rd *RIPS/CAP* IP9 .... 49 F1
Reading Rd *IPNE* IP4 .... 19 G6
Recreation Cl *FX* IP11 .... 42 E4
Recreation La *FX* IP11 .... 42 E4
Recreation Rd *SMKT* IP14 .... 4 D3
Recreation Wy *IPSE* IP3 .... 25 G5
Rectory Fld *RIPS/CAP* IP9 .... 40 C4
Rectory HI *RCOLE* CO7 .... 45 G4
Rectory La *KIR/NAC* IP10 .... 36 E2
  MGTR CO11 .... 46 E4
Rectory Rd *CHTY* IP2 .... 24 B4
Redan St *IP* IP1 .... 2 B1
Red Barn Piece *FRAM/WMKT* IP13 .... 13 H4
Rede La *NHMKT* IP6 .... 11 J2
Redgate La *RIPS/CAP* IP9 .... 32 B4
Red HI *HADL* IP7 .... 29 F1
Redhill Cl *IP* IP1 .... 17 J5
Red Hill Rd *HADL* IP7 .... 29 F2
Red House Cl *FX* IP11 .... 36 D6
Red House Wk *KIR/NAC* IP10 .... 35 F5
Red La *RIPS/CAP* IP9 .... 38 E3
Red Sleeve *RIPS/CAP* IP9 .... 38 D2
Redwing Cl *CHTY* IP2 .... 23 G4
Redwing Dr *SMKT* IP14 .... 5 G2
Redwold Cl *WDBR* IP12 .... 21 K2
Reedland Wy *FX* IP11 .... 42 C5
Reeve Gdns *KESG* IP5 .... 20 D6
Reeve Ldg *FX* IP11 * 42 A1
Regent St *IPNE* IP4 .... 3 H4
  SMKT IP14 .... 4 E2
Regina Cl *IPNE* IP4 .... 25 G2
Reigate Cl *IPSE* IP3 .... 25 G4
Rembrow Rd *RIPS/CAP* IP9 .... 38 E2
Rendlesham Rd *FX* IP11 .... 42 C5
  IP IP1 .... 2 A2
Renfrew Rd *IPNE* IP4 .... 19 G4
Reynolds Av *IPSE* IP3 .... 33 F1
Reynolds Cl *FX* IP11 .... 42 C5
Reynolds Rd *IPSE* IP3 .... 33 F1
Riby Rd *FX* IP11 .... 53 H1
Richardson Rd *RCOLE* CO7 .... 45 H2
Richardsons La *RIPS/CAP* IP9 .... 40 B4
Richmond Rd *IP* IP1 .... 17 J2
Ridgeway *SMKT* IP14 .... 4 C3
Riley Cl *IP* IP1 .... 17 F4
Ringham Rd *IPNE* IP4 .... 25 F1
Risby Cl *IPNE* IP4 .... 25 G1
Ritabrook Rd *CHTY* IP2 .... 23 H6
River HI *RIPW* IP8 .... 17 F4
Riverside *FRAM/WMKT* IP13 .... 14 B2
Riverside Rd *IP* IP1 .... 17 J6
Riverside Vw *FRAM/WMKT* IP13 .... 8 D2
Rivers St *IPNE* IP4 .... 3 K1
Riverview *WDBR* IP12 .... 15 K2
River View Rd *RIPS/CAP* IP9 .... 49 K5
Robeck Rd *IPSE* IP3 .... 24 D6
Robin Cl *SMKT* IP14 .... 5 H4
Robin Dr *CHTY* IP2 .... 23 G4
Rodney Ct *WDBR* IP12 .... 15 K2
Rogers Cl *FX* IP11 .... 42 E4

nderland Rd FX IP11 ....53 F4
nfield Cl IPNE IP4..................25 G1
n La WDBR IP12....................15 H4
nningdale Av IPNE IP4............25 J2
nningdale Dr FX IP11.............43 G4
nray Av FX IP11....................43 G4
rbiton Rd IP IP1....................17 J6
rrey Rd FX IP11....................42 E6
    IP IP1............................23 K1
tton Cl WDBR IP12................15 J4
vallow Cl FX IP11..................43 H3
vallow Dr SMKT IP14...............5 H3
vallow Rd CHTY IP2................23 F4
vallowtail Cl RIPW IP8............31 H1
van Cl KESG IP5....................21 H6
    SMKT IP14.........................4 B3
van Hi RIPW IP8....................22 D5
van La NHMKT IP6.................18 D1
van Meadow RCOLE CO7.........44 A4
vansea Av CHTY IP2...............24 A6
vatchway Cl IPSE IP3.............33 G1
vaynes RCOLE CO7................44 A3
vift Dr SMKT IP14...................5 H3
vinburne Rd IP IP1.................17 H2
vinton Cl CHTY IP2................23 G6
camore Cl RIPW IP8..............23 F6
camore Rd SMKT IP14............5 H1
camore Wy MGTR CO11.........46 D5

T

cket St IPNE IP4......................2 E4
con Rd FX IP11.....................53 G3
kers La SMKT IP14..................5 F5
lboys Cl KESG IP5.................20 D5
lyho Cnr RCOLE CO7.............44 B4
nners Vw IP IP1...................17 J6
nyard Ct WDBR IP12.............15 H5
smania Rd IPNE IP4...............25 J1
nton Cl IP IP1......................18 A1
vern Rd FX IP11....................42 E5
vern St IP IP1.........................2 E3
    SMKT IP14.........................4 E4
nby Rd CHTY IP2..................24 A6
nnyson Cl WDBR IP12...........15 F3
nnyson Cl IPNE IP4..............24 E2
nter Fld RCOLE CO7.............44 B4
rn Rd CHTY IP2....................23 H5
rn Rd FX IP11........................5 G3
e Terrace HADL IP7 *............29 F3
ry Gdns KESG IP5.................21 F6
ackeray Gv SMKT IP14...........4 C1
ackeray Rd IP IP1.................17 H2
anet Rd IPNE IP4..................25 C1
eatre St WDBR IP12..............15 C4
ebe Cl IP IP1.......................17 G5
eberton Rd IPSE IP3.............25 G6
eobald Cl NHMKT IP6..............6 E4
etford Rd IP IP1....................17 J6
irlmere Dr SMKT IP14..............4 C3
stle Cl CHTY IP2....................23 J3
omas Arne Cl SMKT IP14........4 D1
omas Av FX IP11..................42 B2
omas Crs KESG IP5..............26 E1
omas Walls Cl
    FRAM/WMKT IP13.............13 J3
omas Young Cl SMKT IP14.......4 E6
ompson Cl FRAM/WMKT IP13...13 J3
ompson Rd IP IP1.................17 J5
ong Hall Rd FRAM/WMKT IP13...8 B3
ornbush La RIPW IP8............16 C5
orney Green Rd SMKT IP14......5 H1
orney Rd RIPS/CAP IP9.........38 E1
ornhayes Cl CHTY IP2...........23 K4
ornhill NHMKT IP6................11 F1
ornley Dr IPNE IP4...............19 G5
ornley Rd FX IP11................43 H5
orn Wy FX IP11....................42 D6
e Thoroughfare WDBR IP12.....15 F4
orpe La FX IP11....................36 C6
readneedle St HADL IP7.........28 E4
    RCOLE CO7........................44 D6
rough Duncans WDBR IP12....15 F5
rough Jollys KESG IP5...........20 E5
urleston La IP IP1.................11 J6
urlow Ct SMKT IP14................4 E6
urmans La FX IP11................42 A2
urston Ct FX IP11.................42 B6

Tide Mill Wy WDBR IP12..........15 J5
Timperley Cl HADL IP7............28 E3
Timperley Rd HADL IP7...........29 F3
Tinabrook Cl CHTY IP2...........23 H6
Tinker's La HADL IP7..............28 E6
Tintern Cl CHTY IP2................23 K5
Tippet Av SMKT IP14...............4 D1
Titan Ct IP IP1......................17 G5
Titchwell Dr IPSE IP3.............33 J1
Tokio Rd IPNE IP4.................25 F1
Toller Rd IPSE IP3.................24 D4
Toll Gate Rd RIPS/CAP IP9......38 E2
Tolworth Rd IPNE IP4............25 F1
Tomline Ct KIR/NAC IP10........34 C4
Tomline Rd FX IP11...............53 J1
    IPSE IP3............................25 F2
Tommy Flowers Dr KESG IP5....21 F6
Toppesfield Cl HADL IP7.........28 E5
Top Rd FRAM/WMKT IP13........14 C1
Top St WDBR IP12.................21 K1
Tortoiseshell Cl RIPW IP8........31 H4
Tovell's Rd IPNE IP4..............24 E1
Tower Mill La HADL IP7...........29 F4
Tower Mill Rd IP IP1...............17 J6
Tower Ramparts IP IP1.............2 D2
Tower St FX IP11...................53 H1
Tower St IP IP1.......................2 E3
Town Gn SMKT IP14................4 D3
Trafalgar Ct IPNE IP4.............24 E1
Tranmere Gv IP IP1................17 J3
Treetops FX IP11...................42 D3
Treeview SMKT IP14.................4 B3
Trefoil Cl CHTY IP2................23 J3
Tremlett La KESG IP5.............21 G6
Trent Rd IPSE IP3..................24 E5
Trimley Rd KIR/NAC IP10.........36 E3
Trinity Av FX IP11..................52 D1
Trinity Cl KESG IP5................20 A6
    WDBR IP12..........................14 E6
Trinity St IPSE IP3...................3 J7
Trinity Terminal FX IP11 *........52 C1
Troon Gdns IPNE IP4.............19 G5
Truro Crs KESG IP5...............26 E1
Tuddenham Av IPNE IP4...........3 H1
Tuddenham La KESG IP5.........19 G3
Tuddenham Rd IPNE IP4...........3 G1
Tudor Cl RIPS/CAP IP9...........51 G4
Turing Ct KESG IP5................21 F6
Turino Av KESG IP5...............21 K5
Turin St CHTY IP2....................2 E7
Turnbull Ct KESG IP5.............21 F6
Turner Gdns WDBR IP12.........14 E6
Turner Gv KESG IP5...............20 E5
Turner Rd IPSE IP3................33 F1
    SMKT IP14.........................4 C2
Turn La WDBR IP12................15 H5
Turnpike La WDBR IP12..........15 J3
Turret La IPNE IP4...................2 E5
Twelve Acre Ap KESG IP5........20 C6
The Twinnings SMKT IP14.........4 D5
Two Acres RIPS/CAP IP9.........38 E1
Two House Cl FRAM/WMKT IP13...8 D2
Tydemans Ct SMKT IP14..........4 E3
Tye La RIPW IP8....................16 A2
Tylers Gn FX IP11..................42 B3
Tyler St CHTY IP2....................3 F7
Tylers Wy SMKT IP14...............4 E6
Tymmes Pl FRAM/WMKT IP13...14 D1
Tyndale Gdns FX IP11............43 H5
Tyrone Cl IP IP1....................17 G3

U

Ullswater Av FX IP11..............43 J3
Ullswater Rd FRAM/WMKT IP13...9 H3
Ulster Av IP IP1....................17 G4
Undercliff Rd East FX IP11.......43 H6
Undercliff Rd West FX IP11......53 H1
Underhill SMKT IP14................4 D4
Union Rd IPNE IP4...................4 A2
Union St IPNE IP4 *.................3 F3
Union St East SMKT IP14..........4 E3
Union St West SMKT IP14.........4 E3
Unity Rd SMKT IP14.................4 E4
Unity St IPSE IP3....................3 J7
Upland Rd IPNE IP4...............25 F1
Upper Barclay St IPNE IP4........3 F4
Upper Brook St IPNE IP4..........2 E4
Upperfield Dr FX IP11.............43 G4
Upper High St IP IP1................2 D1
Upper Moorfield Rd WDBR IP12...15 H3
Upper Orwell St IPNE IP4..........3 F4
Upper St RCOLE CO7..............44 A4
Upsons Wy KESG IP5.............21 F5
Upton Cl IPNE IP4...................3 J3
Uvedale Gdns NHMKT IP6.........7 F5
Uxbridge Crs IPSE IP3............25 H6

V

Vale La RIPS/CAP IP9.............47 H1
Valiant Rd KESG IP5...............21 H6
Valley Cl IP IP1.....................18 B4
    MGTR CO11.........................46 D4
Valley Farm La HADL IP7.........29 J5
Valley Farm Rd WDBR IP12......15 J4
Valley La RIPS/CAP IP9...........31 J5
Valley Rd IP IP1....................18 A5
Valleyview Dr IPNE IP4...........26 A3
Valley View Ri WDBR IP12........21 K2
Valley Wk FX IP11..................42 E6
Vandyck Rd FX IP11...............33 F1
Vaughan St CHTY IP2..............2 E7
Ventris Cl CHTY IP2...............23 G2
Vere Gdns IP IP1..................18 B3
Vermont Crs IPNE IP4..............3 G1
Vermont Rd IPNE IP4...............3 G1
Verneuil Av SMKT IP14.............4 D6
Vernon St CHTY IP2.................2 D7
Veyses End RCOLE CO7..........44 B3
Vicarage Cl RIPW IP8.............16 E4
Vicarage Hi WDBR IP12..........15 H4
Vicarage La RIPS/CAP IP9.......32 A4
    RIPW IP8............................16 E4
Vicarage Rd FX IP11..............53 H1
    SMKT IP14.........................5 F2
    WDBR IP12.........................15 H4
Victoria Rd FX IP11...............53 H1
    IP IP1................................2 A2
Victoria St FX IP11................43 F6
Victor Vls MGTR CO11 *..........46 A5
Victory Rd IPNE IP4...............19 F6
View Point Rd FX IP11............53 F5
Viking Cl WDBR IP12..............21 K3
Viking Hts WDBR IP12............21 K3
Viking Rd SMKT IP14...............4 D4
Vincent Cl IP IP1...................17 H5
Vincent Drift KESG IP5............21 G5
Vinery Cl FRAM/WMKT IP13.......8 D3
Violet Cl CHTY IP2.................23 J3
Violet Hill Rd SMKT IP14...........4 D2

W

Wades Gv KESG IP5...............21 F6
Wade's La RIPS/CAP IP9.........41 H5
Wadgate Rd FX IP11..............42 D6
Wadhurst Rd IPSE IP3............25 J4
Waggoners Ct WDBR IP12.......15 G4
Wainwright Gdns NHMKT IP6....10 C1
Wainwright Wy KESG IP5.........20 E5
Walker Cha KESG IP5.............26 D1
Walker Cl IPSE IP3................25 H2
The Walk FX IP11..................42 D5
    IP IP1................................2 E3
    KESG IP5...........................20 C5
Wallace Rd IP IP1.................17 H5
Waller's Gv CHTY IP2.............23 J3
Walnut Cl FX IP11.................43 J3
Walnuts La FRAM/WMKT IP13.....8 C4
Walnut Tree Cl RIPW IP8.........16 D3
Walnut Tree La RIPS/CAP IP9....49 K5
Waltham Cl CHTY IP2.............23 K5
Walton Av FX IP11.................52 E1
Walton Cl SMKT IP14...............4 C1
Wardley Cl CHTY IP2..............23 G6
Ward Rd RIPW IP8.................22 E5
Wards Vw KESG IP5...............21 F5
Wareham Av IPSE IP3.............25 J4
Warren Cha KESG IP5.............21 F6
Warren Heath Av IPSE IP3........25 J5
Warren Heath Rd IPSE IP3........25 J5
Warren Hill Rd WDBR IP12.......15 F5
Warren La KESG IP5...............21 H6
    RIPS/CAP IP9......................50 C2
Warrington Rd IP IP1..............18 A4
Warwick Av WDBR IP12...........15 G3
Warwick Rd IPNE IP4...............3 J2
Wash La NHMKT IP6...............12 A2
    SMKT IP14.........................4 B4
Waterford Rd IP IP1...............17 G3
Waterloo Rd IP IP1................17 K6
Waterworks St IPNE IP4............3 G4
Watery La FRAM/WMKT IP13....14 B1
Waveney Rd FX IP11..............53 G1
    IP IP1................................17 H5
Wayside Cl SMKT IP14.............4 E6
Weaver Cl IP IP1...................17 G5
Weavers Cl HADL IP7.............28 E4
    SMKT IP14.........................4 D6
Weavers Wy NHMKT IP6..........10 E2
Webb Rd SMKT IP14................4 E6
Webbs Ct KESG IP5...............20 D6

Weir Pl KIR/NAC IP10.............36 E2
Welbeck Cl FX IP11................42 B3
Wellesley Rd IPNE IP4............24 E2
Wellington Rd HAR CO12.........52 A4
Wellington St IP IP1.................2 A1
Wells Cl IPNE IP4....................3 H3
Wendy Cl RIPS/CAP IP9..........40 D4
Wenham La RCOLE CO7..........38 A3
Wenham Rd RIPW IP8.............30 A2
Wentworth Cl HADL IP7...........29 G5
Wentworth Dr FX IP11.............43 H4
    RIPW IP8............................23 F5
Wesel Av FX IP11..................53 F1
Wesley Wy FX IP11................17 J6
Westbourne Rd IP IP1.............17 J4
Westbury Rd IPNE IP4............19 G5
West End Rd IP IP1..................2 B5
Westerfield Ct IPNE IP4 *.........18 C6
Westerfield Rd IPNE IP4............3 F1
    NHMKT IP6..........................18 C3
Western Av FX IP11................43 J4
Western Cl IPNE IP4...............26 A3
Western's End MGTR CO11.......46 D5
Westgate St IP IP1...................2 D3
Westholme Cl WDBR IP12........15 G5
Westholme Rd IP IP1..............17 K4
Westland KESG IP5................21 H6
West Lawn IPNE IP4...............19 G5
Westleton Wy FX IP11............42 C5
West Mdw IP IP1...................17 F1
West Mill Gdn RIPS/CAP IP9....39 H5
Westminster Rd FX IP11..........25 G2
Westmorland Rd FX IP11.........43 J3
West Rd IPSE IP3..................33 K1
West St HAR CO12.................52 A4
West Vw SMKT IP14.................4 C3
Westwood Av IP IP1...............17 K5
Wetherby Cl IP IP1................18 A2
Wexford Rd IP IP1.................17 G3
Weymouth Rd IPNE IP4...........24 E1
W Francis Vls MGTR CO11 *.....46 B6
Wharfedale Rd IP IP1.............17 K4
Whatfield Wy SMKT IP14...........5 F6
The Wheelwrights FX IP11........42 B2
Wherry La IPNE IP4 *...............3 F5
Wherry Quay IPNE IP4.............3 F5
Wherstead Rd CHTY IP2..........24 B5
Whights' Cnr RIPW IP8...........22 D6
Whinchat Cl CHTY IP2............23 G4
Whincroft FRAM/WMKT IP13......8 D4
Whinfield KESG IP5................21 H6
Whinfield Ct KESG IP5............21 H5
The Whinneys KESG IP5..........20 E5
Whinyard Wy FX IP11.............43 J3
Whitby Rd IPNE IP4...............18 E5
White Elm St IPSE IP3..............3 J6
White Foot La
    FRAM/WMKT IP13.............13 J1
White Horse Cl FX IP11...........43 H4
White Horse Rd RCOLE CO7.....45 H4
    RIPS/CAP IP9......................39 F2
Whitehouse Cots FX IP11 *.......43 H3
White House Rd IP IP1............17 F2
Whites Fld RCOLE CO7............45 F2
Whitethorn Rd IPSE IP3...........26 A6
Whitland Cl CHTY IP2.............31 K1
Whittle Rd CHTY IP2..............23 J1
Whitton Church La IP IP1.........17 H1
Whitton Leyer RIPW IP8..........17 F3
Whitton Pk IP IP1 *................11 K6
Whitworth Cl CHTY IP2...........23 G5
Wickhambrook Ct FX IP11........42 B6
Wicklow Rd IP IP1.................17 G3
Widgeon Cl CHTY IP2.............23 J4
Wigmore Cl CHTY IP2.............23 J6
Wilberforce St IP IP1................2 A2
Wilderness La WDBR IP12........15 H3
Wilding Dr KESG IP5..............20 E6
Wilding Rd RIPW IP8..............22 E6
Wilford Bridge Sp WDBR IP12...15 K2
Wilkinson Dr KESG IP5............26 D1
Wilkinson Wy WDBR IP12........15 H3
Willets Pond RCOLE CO7.........45 J4
William Booth Wy FX IP11........42 C5
Williamsport Wy NHMKT IP6.......7 G6
William St IP IP1.....................2 E2
Willoughby Rd CHTY IP2...........2 C6
Willow Cl NHMKT IP6..............11 F1
Willowcroft Rd IP IP1..............17 K3
The Willows KESG IP5.............19 K4
Willow Tree Cl
    FRAM/WMKT IP13...............8 C3
Wilmslow Av WDBR IP12.........15 F4
Wilmslow Dr CHTY IP2............23 F5
Wilson Rd HADL IP7...............29 F5
    RIPW IP8............................22 E6
Wimborne Av IPSE IP3............25 J3
Wimpole Cl KESG IP5.............26 A1
Wincanton Cl IPNE IP4............19 F4

Winchester CI *SMKT* IP14............4 C3
Winchester Gdns *NHMKT* IP6......11 G1
Winchester Wy *CHTY* IP2............31 J1
Windermere CI *IPSE* IP3.............33 G1
Windermere Rd *FX* IP11.............43 J3
   SMKT IP14.................................4 D3
Winding Piece *RIPS/CAP* IP9......38 E2
Windmill HI *RIPS/CAP* IP9..........38 C2
Windrush Rd *KESG* IP5...............20 D5
Windsor Rd *FX* IP11...................53 G1
   IP IP1...17 J6
Winfrith Rd *IPSE* IP3.................25 J3
Wingfield St *IPNE* IP4.................3 F4
Winston Av *IPNE* IP4..................19 H5
Winston CI *FX* IP11....................42 C5
Withipoll St *IPNE* IP4..................3 F2
Witnesham La *NHMKT* IP6.........12 B6
Witney CI *IPSE* IP3....................33 H1
Wolsey Gdns *FX* IP11.................53 J1
Wolsey Rd *SMKT* IP14.................4 D2
Wolsey St *IP* IP1.........................2 D5
Wolton Rd *KESG* IP5..................20 D6
Wolves Farm La *HADL* IP7..........29 H2
Woodbridge Rd
   FRAM/WMKT IP13..................13 H2

IPNE IP4.....................................3 H3
   KESG IP5..................................20 A5
Woodbridge Rd East *IPNE* IP4...19 H6
Woodcock Rd *CHTY* IP2.............23 H5
Wood Farm Rd
   FRAM/WMKT IP13..................12 E4
Woodfield Dr *SMKT* IP14..............4 E4
Woodfield La *RIPS/CAP* IP9........48 A5
   SMKT IP14.................................4 E4
Woodgates Rd *RCOLE* CO7.........38 B6
Woodhouse La *KIR/NAC* IP10.....26 D5
Woodhouse Sq *IPNE* IP4..............3 G4
Woodlands *HADL* IP7.................28 C3
   RIPS/CAP IP9..........................40 C3
Woodlands Wy *RIPW* IP8............16 E1
Woodlark Dr *SMKT* IP14..............5 G2
Woodpecker CI *SMKT* IP14...........5 H4
Woodpecker Rd *CHTY* IP2...........23 G4
Woodrush Rd *IPSE* IP3...............25 K5
Woodside *KESG* IP5...................21 K5
Wood Side *SMKT* IP14..................4 C4
Woodspring CI *CHTY* IP2.............23 K5
Woodstone Av *IP* IP1.................18 B4
Woods La *WDBR* IP12.................15 H2
Woods Wk *KESG* IP5...................26 E1

Woodthorpe CI *HADL* IP7............29 G5
Woodthorpe Rd *HADL* IP7...........29 F5
Woodville Rd *IPNE* IP4.................4 K4
Woollards CI *IP* IP1...................23 K1
Woolmers CI *SMKT* IP14...............4 E5
Woolner CI *HADL* IP7.................29 F5
   NHMKT IP6..............................11 F2
Woolnough Rd *WDBR* IP12.........15 G3
The Woolnoughs *KESG* IP5.........20 E6
Woolverstone CI *CHTY* IP2..........23 G6
Wootton Dr *IP* IP1.....................18 B5
Worcester Rd *IPSE* IP3...............33 F1
Wordsworth Crs *IP* IP1..............17 H2
Wordsworth Rd *SMKT* IP14...........4 C1
Workshop La *KIR/NAC* IP10........34 C4
Worsley CI *CHTY* IP2.................23 G5
Wren Av *CHTY* IP2.....................23 G4
Wren CI *SMKT* IP14.....................5 H4
Wrens Pk *FX* IP11.....................43 J3
Wright CI *SMKT* IP14....................4 E6
Wright La *KESG* IP5...................20 E5
Wright Rd *IPSE* IP3...................25 H5
Wroxham Rd *IPSE* IP3................24 E4
Wye Rd *IPSE* IP3.......................25 F4
Wykes Bishop St *IPSE* IP3............3 H6

Wynterton CI *IPSE* IP3...............25
   WDBR IP12................................15
Wynton Ri *SMKT* IP14...................5
Wyvern Rd *IPSE* IP3...................25

Y

Yarmouth Rd *IP* IP1...................23
   WDBR IP12................................15
Yeoman Crs *HADL* IP7................29
Yeoman Rd *FX* IP11....................53
Yeoman Wy *HADL* IP7.................29
Yew Ct *CHTY* IP2.......................23
Yewtree Gv *KESG* IP5.................20
Yew Tree Ri *FRAM/WMKT* IP13.....8
Yewtree Ri *RIPW* IP8.................23
York Crs *NHMKT* IP6..................11
York Rd *FX* IP11........................43
   IPSE IP3...................................25
   KESG IP5..................................27

Index - featured places

The Abbey School
   WDBR IP12................................15 H4
Abbots Hall Primary School
   SMKT IP14...................................4 D4
Alnesbourne Priory Golf Club
   KIR/NAC IP10..........................33 H4
Alpha Business Park
   IP IP1..17 H2
Alton Water Sports Centre
   RIPS/CAP IP9..........................48 D4
Amberfield School
   KIR/NAC IP10..........................34 D3
Ancient House
   IP IP1..2 E3
Barn Business Centre
   RCOLE CO7..............................45 J1
Bartlet Hospital
   FX IP11....................................43 G6
BBC Radio Suffolk
   IP IP1..2 C2
Beacon Hill Special School
   CHTY IP2..................................23 J4
Bealings School
   FRAM/WMKT IP13..................20 E1
Beaumont Primary School
   HADL IP7.................................28 E3
Belstead School
   RIPW IP8.................................23 F5
Bentley Primary School
   RIPS/CAP IP9..........................39 K4
Birchwood County
   Primary School
   KESG IP5..................................21 H6
Blackfriars Priory Hall
   IPNE IP4.....................................3 F4
Bosmere Primary School
   NHMKT IP6................................6 D5
The Brackenbury
   Sports Centre
   FX IP11....................................43 H5
Bramford CE Primary School
   RIPW IP8.................................16 D4
Brantham Athletic
   & Social Club
   MGTR CO11.............................46 C6
Brewery Museum
   IPSE IP3...................................24 D4
Bridge Trading Estate
   NHMKT IP6..............................10 E2
Britannia Primary School
   IPNE IP4.................................25 G2
Broke Hall Primary School
   IPNE IP4.................................25 K2
Brook Craft Market
   IPNE IP4.....................................2 E3
Brookhouse Business Park
   CHTY IP2..................................23 J1
Brooklands Primary School
   MGTR CO11.............................46 D5
Broom Hill Swimming Pool
   IP IP1..17 K5
Broomvale Business Centre
   RIPW IP8.................................10 D4
Bucklesham Primary School
   KIR/NAC IP10..........................35 J1
Buttermarket Shopping Centre
   IP IP1..2 E4

Capel St Mary CE
   Primary School
   RIPS/CAP IP9..........................38 E2
The Card Centre
   FX IP11....................................43 F5
Cardinal Retail Park
   IP IP1..2 D5
Castle Hill J&I School
   IP IP1..17 K2
Causton Junior School
   FX IP11....................................42 D4
Cedars Hotel
   SMKT IP14...................................5 G5
Cedarwood Primary School
   KESG IP5..................................26 D1
Chantry Clinic
   CHTY IP2..................................23 H4
Chantry High School
   CHTY IP2..................................23 J4
Chelmondiston CP School
   RIPS/CAP IP9..........................40 D4
Chilton Community
   Primary School
   SMKT IP14...................................4 D2
Christchurch Mansion
   IPNE IP4.....................................3 F2
UGC Cinema
   IP IP1..2 C5
Civil Service Sports Club
   KIR/NAC IP10..........................26 D6
Claydon Business Park
   NHMKT IP6..............................10 D1
Claydon Country House Hotel
   NHMKT IP6..............................10 E3
Claydon High School
   NHMKT IP6..............................11 F3
Claydon Primary School
   NHMKT IP6..............................11 F2
Cliff Lane Primary School
   IPSE IP3...................................24 D4
Clifford Road Primary School
   IPSE IP3...................................24 E2
Colneis Junior School
   FX IP11....................................43 G4
Combs Ford Primary School
   SMKT IP14...................................5 F5
Combs Middle School
   SMKT IP14...................................5 F6
Copdock CC
   RIPW IP8.................................30 C2
Copdock Primary School
   RIPW IP8.................................30 C1
Copleston High School
   IPNE IP4.................................25 H2
Corn Exchange
   HADL IP7.................................28 E5
Corn Exchange & Film Theatre
   IP IP1..2 D3
Courtyard by Marriott Hotel
   IPSE IP3...................................33 K2
Creeting St Mary
   Primary School
   NHMKT IP6..................................7 G1
Crown Pools
   IP IP1..2 D2
Dale Hall Primary School
   IP IP1..18 A3

Deben High School
   FX IP11....................................42 E6
Deben Swimming Pool
   WDBR IP12................................15 H5
East Bergholt CE
   Primary School
   RCOLE CO7..............................45 F2
East Bergholt High School
   RCOLE CO7..............................45 H1
Eastgate Shopping Centre
   IPNE IP4.....................................3 F3
Electric Palace Cinema
   HAR CO12................................52 A4
Elizabeth Orwell Hotel
   FX IP11....................................43 G5
Elton Park Business Centre
   CHTY IP2..................................23 H1
Elton Park Industrial Estate
   CHTY IP2..................................23 H1
Euro Retail Park
   IPSE IP3...................................25 J6
Fairfield Infant School
   FX IP11....................................43 F5
Farlingaye High School
   WDBR IP12................................15 F3
Farthing Road Industrial
   Estate
   IP IP1..17 G6
Feliwstowe Leisure Centre
   FX IP11....................................53 H1
Felixstowe and Walton FC
   FX IP11....................................43 F4
Felixstowe Cemetery
   FX IP11....................................42 D6
Felixstowe College
   FX IP11....................................43 H6
Felixstowe Ferry Golf Club
   FX IP11....................................43 K3
Felixstowe General Hospital
   FX IP11....................................43 F6
Felixstowe Pier
   FX IP11....................................53 J1
Felixstowe RFC
   FX IP11....................................53 G1
Flatford Bridge Cottage (NT)
   RCOLE CO7..............................45 H6
Fore Street Pool
   IP IP1..3 G5
Foxhall Heath Stadium
   IPNE IP4.................................26 B2
Fozel Theatre
   HADL IP7.................................28 D5
The Framlingham
   Swimming Club
   WDBR IP12................................15 H5
Gainsborough Sports Centre
   IPSE IP3...................................33 G1
Ganges Museum
   RIPS/CAP IP9..........................51 J5
Gorseland Primary School
   KESG IP5..................................21 G5
Industrial Centre
   CHTY IP2....................................2 E6
Grange Primary School
   HADL IP7.................................42 C6
Greenwich Business Park
   IPSE IP3...................................24 D4

Grundisburgh County
   Primary School
   FRAM/WMKT IP13..................13
Gulpher Business Park
   FX IP11....................................42
Gusford Primary School
   CHTY IP2..................................23
Hadleigh Business Park
   HADL IP7.................................29
Hadleigh Health Centre
   HADL IP7.................................28
Hadleigh High School
   HADL IP7.................................29
Hadleigh Primary School
   HADL IP7.................................28
Hadleigh Road
   Industrial Estate
   CHTY IP2..................................23
Hadleigh RUFC
   HADL IP7.................................28
Hadleigh Swimming Pool
   HADL IP7.................................28
Halifax Primary School
   CHTY IP2..................................24
Handford Hall Primary
   School
   IP IP1..23
Harwich Community
   Primary School
   HAR CO12................................52
Harwich Primary School
   HAR CO12................................52
Harwich Redoubt Fort
   HAR CO12................................52
Harwich Town Sailing Club
   HAR CO12................................52
Heath Primary School
   KESG IP5..................................20
Heathside Special School
   IPNE IP4.................................25
Hillside Community
   Primary School
   CHTY IP2..................................24
Hill View Business Park
   NHMKT IP6..............................11
HM Customs & Excise
   IPNE IP4.....................................2
Holbrook CP School
   RIPS/CAP IP9..........................49
Holbrook High School
   RIPS/CAP IP9..........................49
Holywells High School
   IPSE IP3...................................25
The Hotel Elizabeth
   RIPW IP8.................................30
Ipswich Airport (disused)
   IPSE IP3...................................33
Ipswich Crematorium
   IPNE IP4.................................18
Ipswich Golf Club
   IPSE IP3...................................26
Ipswich High School
   RIPS/CAP IP9..........................40
Ipswich Hospital
   IPNE IP4.................................25
Ipswich Museum
   IP IP1..2

Acknowledgements

Schools address data provided by Education Direct.

Petrol station information supplied by Johnsons.

Garden centre information provided by:

Garden Centre Association ● Britains best garden centres

🌷 Wyevale Garden Centres

The statement on the front cover of this atlas is sourced, selected and quoted
from a reader comment and feedback form received in 2004

AA **Street by Street** QUESTIONNAIRE

Dear Atlas User
Your comments, opinions and recommendations are very important to us.
So please help us to improve our street atlases by taking a few minutes
to complete this simple questionnaire.

You do not need a stamp (unless posted outside the UK). If you do not want to remove
this page from your street atlas, then photocopy it or write your answers on a plain sheet
of paper.

Send to: Marketing Assistant, AA Publishing, 14th Floor Fanum House,
Freepost SCE 4598, Basingstoke RG21 4GY

ABOUT THE ATLAS...

Please state which city / town / county you bought:

_____

Where did you buy the atlas? (City, Town, County)

_____

For what purpose? (please tick all applicable)

To use in your local area ☐   **To use on business or at work** ☐

Visiting a strange place ☐   **In the car** ☐   **On foot** ☐

Other (please state)

_____

Have you ever used any street atlases other than AA Street by Street?

Yes ☐   No ☐

If so, which ones?

_____

Is there any aspect of our street atlases that could be improved?
(Please continue on a separate sheet if necessary)

_____
_____
_____
_____

ML143z

continued overleaf

Please list the features you found most useful:

_____

_____

_____

Please list the features you found least useful:

_____

_____

_____

LOCAL KNOWLEDGE...

Local knowledge is invaluable. Whilst every attempt has been made to make the information contained in this atlas as accurate as possible, should you notice any inaccuracies, please detail them below (if necessary, use a blank piece of paper) or e-mail us at *streetbystreet@theAA.com*

_____

_____

_____

ABOUT YOU...

Name (Mr/Mrs/Ms)

Address

                                        Postcode

Daytime tel no

E-mail address

Which age group are you in?

Under 25 ☐   25-34 ☐   35-44 ☐   45-54 ☐   55-64 ☐   65+ ☐

Are you an AA member?   YES ☐   NO ☐

Do you have Internet access?   YES ☐   NO ☐

Thank you for taking the time to complete this questionnaire. Please send it to us as soon as possible, and remember, you do not need a stamp (unless posted outside the UK).

We may use information we hold about you to, telephone or email you about other products and services offered by the AA, we do NOT disclose this information to third parties.

Please tick here if you do not wish to hear about products and services from the AA. ☐